HOW TO DO HARD THINGS

Written and Illustrated by

VERONICA DEARLY

INTRODUCTION
LIFE IS HARD

It's also pretty magical. It's full of ups, downs, loop-the-loops, and then, like a roller coaster, it's suddenly over and you have to get off.

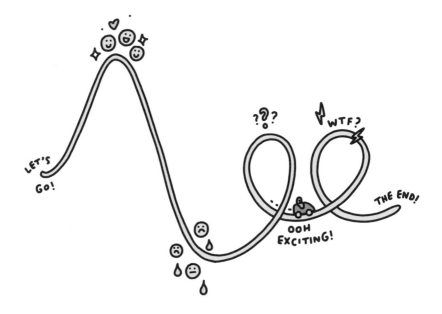

And that's life. What a wild ride.

But as hard as it is, you won't find me complaining. Well... I mean you probably will occasionally, and that's fine. That's part of life, too.

This is a book about **actual real life**, some reflections on all the wonderful and terrible things we might find difficult, and advice on how to handle them. It's about overcoming obstacles—big and small—so you can go on to make your actual real life a tiny bit more like living the dream every single day.

LIFE IS COMPLICATED

When you look at all the different things that make up your life, as I have tried to do here, it becomes quite clear why it feels so bloody overwhelming sometimes.

Whether it is chores at home or stress at work, maintaining friendships or managing your finances, there's **always** so much to do. So many little pieces of life to try and stay on top of. Some are big, some are small. Some bits you will find super easy, and other bits you will studiously ignore and pretend they don't even exist because you just can't face up to dealing with them.

you MIGHT FIND IT _really hard_ TO DO SOMETHING THAT YOU SEE OTHER PEOPLE DO _effortlessly_ EVERY DAY, BUT YOU KNOW WHAT, SOMEONE ELSE IS PROBABLY LOOKING AT YOU AND FEELS _exactly the same._

You can have almost all your shit together, but if there are one or two areas of your life that you can't quite get the hang of, then it can easily feel like nothing is working. This is especially true if the area you are struggling with feels like the most important one in the world.

the VERONICA DEARLY WHEEL OF LIFE

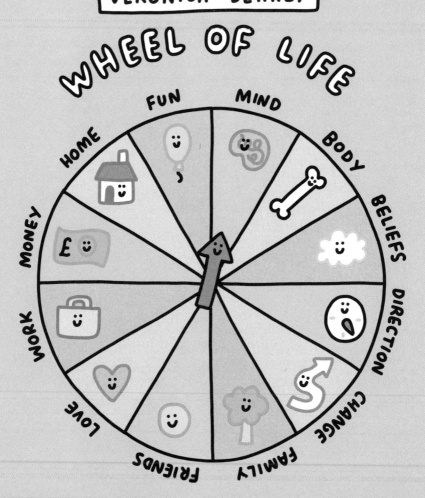

Actual real life CAN FEEL COMPLICATED, AND THAT'S BECAUSE IT _IS_ COMPLICATED. IT'S GOT *lots* OF MOVING PARTS, AND THEY *all* COMBINE + AFFECT EACH OTHER.

Unfortunately, one of the many hard things in life is learning to say "Excuse me, I'm finding this really hard."

This book encourages you to acknowledge the things that feel difficult to you. It doesn't matter if everyone else seems to find them easy. This book understands that for every tiny little thing that feels easy to one person, there will be someone else feeling like that particular tiny little thing is **just too hard**.

It doesn't expect you to know how to do something already without having ever been taught. This book is here to help you! It doesn't want to judge you or make you feel all embarrassed. It wants to make the hard bits of your life just a little bit easier.

This book would also like to remind you that you are not the only person in the world who finds things difficult.

This book is a journey through what I hope is a rather comprehensive breakdown of your life, a look at what you are already absolutely brilliant at, and how you can do those things that right now feel like they're just too hard.

Above all, it is here to politely but firmly remind you that **you can do hard things.**

YOU CAN DO HARD THINGS

(BUT ONLY AFTER YOU'VE TOTALLY FREAKED OUT ABOUT THEM. ONCE YOU'VE DONE THAT YOU SHOULD BE JUST FINE.)

HOW DO I USE THIS BOOK?

I mean, it's a book, and it's yours now to do whatever the heck you want with it. I've written it as though it is a gentle, meandering exploration of your life, with lots of interactive pages for you to complete and, hopefully, enjoy.

You can flick through to find a specific chapter that speaks to you, work through methodically from front to back, or open it at random and see what you learn.

MY TOP TIPS FOR USING THIS BOOK ARE SIMILAR TO MY TIPS FOR LIFE IN GENERAL...

TOP TIPS

☑ TAKE IT AT YOUR OWN PACE.

☑ ENJOY THE JOURNEY.

☑ REMEMBER: YOU CAN DO HARD THINGS!

CHAPTER 1

MIND

I TRIED TO USE UP MY EMOTIONS BUT THEY JUST KEEP COMING

FEELING YOUR FEELINGS

We spend a lot of time being told to push our emotions down and pretend we don't feel them, so it's no wonder we tend to do just that. We say, "I'm fine, I'm okay."

Even when we are really absolutely **not** okay. Even when the person asking you can tell you aren't okay, it's still somehow easier to pretend you are to avoid an awkward conversation where you actually acknowledge that you aren't a robot person.

However, emotions are just a part of being a human being, and the more we squash them down, the more likely it is that they will blow up in our faces.

It's a bit like when you don't want to take the bin bag out, so you just push it down more and more and keep adding to it, and eventually it explodes out of the top when you try and put more in it, and then the bag bursts on the way out of the kitchen when you finally do give in and change it, and there's just trash and bin juice everywhere and you have nothing left but regrets and a big mess to clear up.

Now, I am pretty sure I'm not alone in hating bin juice, so I have been doing my absolute best to avoid this where possible.

HOW I USED TO TREAT MY EMOTIONS

Instead of thinking of my emotions as rubbish I need to throw away, I have started to think of them as lovely fluffy animals coming to visit. Some I am more comfortable with than others, sure—welcoming sadness up onto the sofa is never going to be easy. But it's probably a lot easier than dealing with having an actual full-size llama on the sofa, so there is that.

Good, bad, or kind of neutral, emotions are all there for a good reason. Sometimes you have to sit with them a while rather than pretending they don't exist.

Take a look at your feelings and think about ways you can welcome them all, give them the time that they need, and maybe even create a little tradition to go with them. We often celebrate feeling happy with cake or bubbles, so setting a little plan for when you feel sad or angry is a great way to feel a bit more ready for them.

HOW I TREAT MY EMOTIONS NOW

OKAY, YOU'RE HERE. LET'S HAVE A LITTLE CRY AND WATCH A ROM-COM, AND WE CAN SEE HOW WE FEEL AFTER THAT.

MY EMOTIONAL RANGE...

EMOTION	HOW I CAN VISUALIZE IT	WHAT I CAN DO WHEN I'M FEELING THAT WAY
E.G. SADNESS	A BIG FLUFFY LLAMA	PUT ON LOVELY FRESH PJ'S + WATCH SITCOMS

MY CAT OF CONTENTMENT

THE DIFFERENCE BETWEEN A GOOD DAY AND A BAD DAY IS ~~YOUR~~ ~~ATTITUDE~~ A LOT MORE COMPLEX THAN A SANCTIMONIOUS "MOTIVATIONAL" QUOTE.

THIS ISN'T A BOOK ABOUT MENTAL HEALTH

… because quite frankly I'm in no way qualified to talk about something so incredibly important. Also, the book would have to be super, super long and there still wouldn't be room for all the other chapters. But I can't have a little chapter about mind without a few little mental health reminders:

I HAVE SUFFERED FROM MENTAL HEALTH PROBLEMS, LIKE APPROX 1 IN 4 PEOPLE IN THE WHOLE ENTIRE WORLD. IF YOU DO TOO, THEN YOU ARE MOST CERTAINLY NOT ALONE.

MENTAL HEALTH PROBLEMS CAN AFFECT YOU REGARDLESS OF WHETHER YOU HAVE AN OUTWARDLY HAPPY OR PERFECT LIFE. THEY ARE NOT A LACK OF GRATITUDE, AND THEY ARE NOT SOMETHING TO FEEL GUILTY ABOUT.

YOUR MENTAL HEALTH IS JUST AS IMPORTANT AS YOUR PHYSICAL HEALTH AND YOU ARE ENTITLED TO PROTECT IT HOWEVER YOU NEED TO.

THERE IS ALWAYS SOMEONE OUT THERE WHO WILL LISTEN - WHETHER IT'S A LOVED ONE, A QUALIFIED PROFESSIONAL, OR SOME RANDOM PERSON ON THE INTERNET. DON'T KEEP IT IN YOUR EMOTIONAL BIN BAG FOR TOO LONG.

And finally…

YOU ARE MORE THAN ENOUGH.

IT'S ALL IN YOUR MIND

THAT MOMENT WHEN YOU REALIZE MINDSET isn't JUST AN ANNOYING BUZZWORD AND YOU ARE, IN FACT, HOLDING YOURSELF BACK.

OH CRAP.

The most annoying part of having some kind of self-awareness is that you can quite clearly see the times when you are responsible for your own misfortune. Unfortunately, it's not always easy to change your mindset, because it's so tied into the way you see the world and how your life has unfolded so far. Ugh, right?

So without being a nightmare person, I just try my best to approach things with a vaguely, loosely positive attitude, and it really does help.

If you look for things to complain about, believe me, you'll find them. Even if you don't look for them, they will show up and get right in your face sometimes. Because there's always some bullshit going on somewhere.

Sometimes, that bullshit will be serious and awful and will absolutely consume you. No amount of "good vibes only" can change that fact. Other times, it's low level, and you can almost ignore it completely.

Overall, it's nice to be positive, but that's not the same as always pretending everything is sunshine and rainbows and being perky all the time. Sometimes, it's just about acknowledging that even though things are terrible, there are some things in your life that aren't terrible.

TAKE A MINUTE TO BE GRATEFUL FOR EVERYTHING THAT ISN'T COMPLETELY SHIT RIGHT NOW

Looking on the bright side is a lovely way to look at the world— just so long as you're not pushing all the negative stuff down into an overflowing emotional bin bag, you're good to go.

WORRIES, FEARS, ANXIETIES-OH MY!

Sometimes, it doesn't matter how much time you put into working on your mindset—you just can't stop the worries popping into your brain.

Overthinking, worrying, and anxiety all exist on a scale from something you can deal with yourself by taking your mind off of things, right up to something all-consuming that you might need to seek professional help for. For the purposes of this book, I'm focusing on the low-level existential anxiety that seems to get into most of our brains from time to time.

Annoyingly, like with most things, sometimes the best way to deal with your fears is also the scariest...

MY BRAIN EVERY DAY:

IT'S A GREAT DAY TO HAVE A ~~GREAT DAY~~ FULL BLOWN EXISTENTIAL CRISIS

JUMP IN AT THE DEEP END

As a child, I always had a real fear of the deep end. Even now, I can still clearly remember being at the side of the swimming pool one day, looking underwater, and seeing that the bottom of the pool was **miles** away. Seriously, in my brain, still to this day, I can see all those little square chequerboard tiles stretching all the way down, at least 30 meters.

Of course, the pool wasn't that deep. I don't really know a lot about swimming, but it was definitely just a regular pool. But because of how anxious I was, my brain was showing me something completely terrifying that reinforced the idea that I was right to be scared. My brain didn't want me to be the sort of person who just swam around in the deep end like it was no big deal—it wanted me clinging to the sides. It wanted me to be safe.

That's a fair enough thought, if you can't swim. But I actually **could**. I wasn't a brilliant swimmer, but I could easily have swam across the pool. Which is lucky, because on this same day, the substitute swimming teacher pushed me into the water. In the deep end.

I was terrified, of course. But I found myself a minute later perfectly fine and treading water. Now, this isn't a story where I suddenly, magically found myself completely free of fear. But from that point, my idea of the deep end slowly started to reflect what was actually happening in real life. I still couldn't touch the bottom of the pool while I swam, but it wasn't actually that scary or far away.

First of all, I just want to say—that swimming teacher was obviously not cool, and my mum was very angry about the whole thing. But despite the fact it was the wrong thing for the teacher to have done, I did learn something. Sometimes you do need to take some kind of plunge and be scared in order to start pushing things around in your brain.

So when your brain starts playing tricks on you to try and keep you safe, think about how you can find your way to the deep end yourself. (And if that's by taking baby steps from the shallow end, that's fine, too.)

HOW TO SWITCH OFF YOUR BRAIN

With so many worries swimming around in there, sometimes it would be nice to be able to just switch off and sleep. If you're anything like me though, your brain reaches peak red-alert levels at around 4am. So working on switching off the brain before bed has been a real game changer for me.

SOME HANDY TIPS I'VE PICKED UP ALONG THE WAY...

DO SOMETHING
RELAXING

BEFORE BED

SO YOU'VE GOT A CHANCE TO UNWIND BEFORE YOU EVEN TRY TO GO TO SLEEP.

BAN YOUR PHONE AFTER LIGHTS OUT

BUT THEN YOU KNOW THIS ALREADY, RIGHT?

DON'T EVEN THINK ABOUT
TRYING TO SLEEP.

JUST FOCUS ON DEEP BREATHING AND RELAXING YOUR BODY. GENTLY RUB YOUR TUMMY AND JUST PRETEND YOU'RE A FLUFFY AND EXTREMELY RELAXED PET. PETS DON'T HAVE ANYTHING TO WORRY ABOUT DO THEY?

CHAPTER 2

BODY

IF MY BODY CAN FIND THE GOODNESS IN POTATO WAFFLES, I CAN FIND THE GOODNESS IN MY BODY.

SELF LOVE, ACCEPTANCE, AND/OR NEUTRALITY

There are a lot of expectations put on how our bodies look and work but also on how we should feel about them. I think by now we are all more than aware that if we could just fall in love with ourselves, body and mind, then we could all live happily ever after. But falling in love with yourself can be much **easier said than done**.

And no wonder! We've spent our whole lives so far being shown images of perfection, sold ways to become more perfect, and reminded frequently that we are just not quite right no matter how bloody hard we try. Those messages cut deep, and it's pretty hard to just suck all of those ideas out of your brain and embrace self-love.

SELF-LOVE IS GREAT BUT IF YOU DON'T FEEL THAT WAY, IT'S NOT JUST ANOTHER THING TO FEEL GUILTY ABOUT.

So instead, let's open our minds to self-acceptance and the different steps we can take to get there. It will mean unlearning some of the lessons we've absorbed over the years and breaking some unhelpful thought patterns. Everybody and every body is different, so it won't mean the same thing for all of us, and that's fine too.

Just like our brains, our bodies are incredibly complicated and made up of lots of different parts, and it's unlikely you'll feel exactly the same about all of it. For example, you might love your sparkly blue eyes, accept that you are always going to have broad shoulders, and feel totally neutral about your knobbly knees because, while they don't look like they belong in *Beautiful Knees Monthly* magazine, you are grateful that they do the job you need them to do.

Check out the scale below, and think about which things about yourself fit on there and where...

THE SCALE OF SELF-ACCEPTANCE

LOVE
THE PARTS (OR MAYBE ALL!) OF YOUR BODY THAT YOU LOVE. THINGS YOU ARE PROUD OF AND MAKE YOU FEEL REALLY GOOD.

THINGS I LOVE ABOUT MYSELF...

ACCEPTANCE
THINGS YOU MIGHT NOT ALWAYS HAVE BEEN VERY FOND OF, BUT NOW YOU'VE COME TO ACCEPT AS BEING PERFECTLY FINE AND O.K.

THINGS I ACCEPT ABOUT MYSELF...

NEUTRALITY
YOU CERTAINLY MIGHT NOT FEEL GREAT ABOUT THESE THINGS, BUT ALSO, YOU DON'T ALWAYS NEED TO... BECAUSE YOUR BODY IS FOR MORE THAN BEING BEAUTIFUL.

THINGS I AM NEUTRAL ABOUT...

LOVE

ACCEPTANCE

NEUTRALITY

BEAUTY STANDARDS

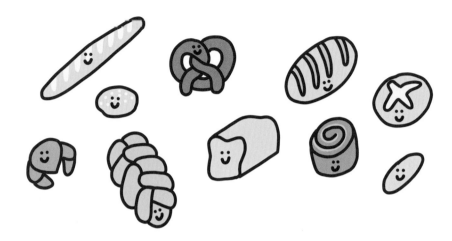

BEAUTY COMES IN ALL SHAPES AND SIZES

We just need to look at the world of bread to see that beauty really does come in all shapes and sizes. It's just that when most of the things being put in front of your eyeballs are slim and white, it's easy to feel like people will only want to eat you if you're a baguette.

More often than not, human nature is telling us that standing out is a bad idea, and we need to fit ourselves into whatever mold we see the most of. Embracing the things about yourself that make you stand out can feel like a daring act in a world that tells us to blend in, but sometimes **standing out** is the only way we can truly feel like ourselves.

BLENDING IN
MIGHT STOP YOU
FROM BEING EATEN,
BUT SO WILL BEING
BOLD + BRIGHT AND
LOOKING LIKE YOU
MIGHT BE A LITTLE
BIT TOXIC.

COMPARISON IS THE THIEF OF ALL JOY

BUT IT'S TOTALLY NORMAL.

When we are constantly pitted against each other and made to feel like there's somehow something wrong with us because of our differences, is it any wonder that we spend a lot of time comparing ourselves and what we look like to other people? Absolutely not.

Can comparison make you utterly miserable? Yes.

But **once again**, is it another one of those many things we are told we shouldn't do but find ourselves doing again and again because it's just so deeply ingrained in us from a young age and then feel even more guilty about? Also yes. (My guilt list, like my to-do list, seems to get longer every single day...)

The best thing you can do when you're comparing yourself to someone and it's making you feel like a bag of crap is to notice it. Accept that it's totally normal, you are not some kind of monster, and then refocus on yourself and the things about yourself that are utterly brilliant, without needing to set someone else as a benchmark.

~~SNAP~~ FUCK JUDGMENTS

Much like comparison, judgment is something we often do instinctively. We can, and do, make snap judgments about people for many reasons, but as this is the Body chapter, that's what I'm focusing on here. We usually judge people based on two things:

#1 OUR OWN INSECURITIES

For example, if you are insecure because you've got massive boobs that you always try to hide and you see someone letting it all hang out, your instant reaction might be "Oh, they shouldn't be wearing that…" But if you had time to reflect, the ideal reaction to seeing someone making their own personal fashion choices would be more like "Yasssss, look at them go!" You have an insecurity—welcome to the club. We all do. And that's totally fine. But projecting our insecurities onto other people isn't fine.

#2 BECAUSE THEY CHALLENGE SOMETHING THAT WE TELL OURSELVES

For example, you see someone running past your house at 6am and think "Look at them running around in their fancy running gear pretending that they actually like running—how smug." And when I say "you," I actually mean "me." Because that was something I used to feel a lot. I told myself that running is too hard, running is for jerks, and anyone who buys nice running clothes is literally the worst. The people running past my house challenged me because, deep down, I knew I wanted to do it too, but couldn't be bothered. Judging people for doing something I told myself I couldn't do was much easier than facing up to the fact that that is a huge lie. And now I love running. Life, what a wild ride.

Judging people is just another way our brains are trying to keep us safe from facing up to our fears or pushing ourselves out of our comfort zones. But how do we actually stop projecting our insecurities around a particular thing? Ask yourself these questions to scrutinize your common judgments.

THINGS I FIND MYSELF BEING JUDGMENTAL ABOUT...

RUNNERS

WHAT COULD BE TRIGGERING THAT REACTION?

SECRET
RUNNING
JEALOUSY

☺ A DIFFERENT WAY OF THINKING ABOUT IT... ☺

GOOD FOR
THEM! MAYBE
I SHOULD TRY IT

If you've been brought up to believe that people with tattoos are all evil, or that all people who wear sandals and socks are evil, or any of the infinite number of horrible things people are led to believe, then it might take time to turn off that reflex. But I promise you, you can do it and you will feel much better for it. Judging people less allows more space in your life for things that are generally a lot more pleasant than criticizing others (which is basically most other things).

STOP PROJECTING YOUR INSECURITIES AROUND A PARTICULAR THING

FEEL THE **NEGATIVITY** AROUND THAT THING SLIGHTLY DECREASE

FEEL LESS COMPELLED TO **JUDGE** OTHER PEOPLE ABOUT THAT THING

FEEL MORE LIKE MAYBE IF YOU AREN'T JUDGING THAT THING IN OTHER PEOPLE, MAYBE THEY **AREN'T JUDGING YOU ABOUT IT** EITHER

FEEL THE INSECURITY **GRADUALLY MELT AWAY**

SPEND MORE TIME BEING A BADASS

YOU ARE ~~WHAT YOU EAT~~ SO MUCH MORE THAN WHAT YOU DECIDE TO PUT IN YOUR BODY

Some ways of life, diets, or restrictions may really appeal to you and work well for you. Equally, you might try those things, and even though you really want them to be the perfect fit, you find that actually they make you feel like crap. I'm not going to presume to second-guess anything about your body, but, deep down, you probably know if you've found your flow when it comes to food and drink or if you could do with a bit of a change.

  Sobriety might be a non-negotiable for your physical and mental health, regardless of what your peers think about it.

Veganism might be an ethical decision based on your personal beliefs.

Indulging in foods that other people think are too greasy, too fancy, or too childish might bring you joy.

Intuitive eating might work perfectly for you or you might prefer the structure of a nutritionally balanced weekly meal plan.

You may dip in and out of different things for a long time before you find a way of fueling your brilliant body that makes you feel good. **That's very normal.** And this way of thinking doesn't just apply to diet and food. It applies to exercise, makeup, fashion, and all sorts of other things about your body. Ultimately, the only person you need to keep happy and healthy with your choices is you.

YOUR BODY, YOUR RULES

There are so many ways to measure yourself as a person. Measuring yourself by how much you weigh is one of my least favorite. How far and fast you can run or how many likes your selfie gets are also not very helpful. Here are some other ideas for your perusal…

RULERS I COULD USE TO MEASURE MYSELF...

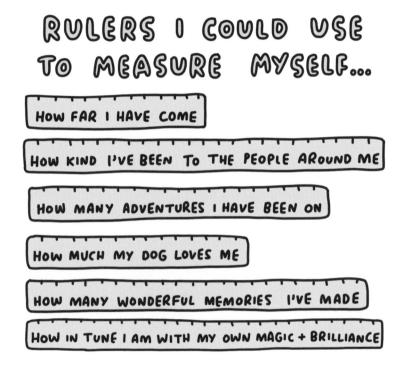

HOW FAR I HAVE COME

HOW KIND I'VE BEEN TO THE PEOPLE AROUND ME

HOW MANY ADVENTURES I HAVE BEEN ON

HOW MUCH MY DOG LOVES ME

HOW MANY WONDERFUL MEMORIES I'VE MADE

HOW IN TUNE I AM WITH MY OWN MAGIC + BRILLIANCE

But like everything, especially when it comes to your body, you need to come up with your own measurements.

There is so much noise, and so much unsolicited advice, about how to make yourself more beautiful, slim, healthy, or generally better in some way than you already are. You need to ignore almost all of it, and just focus on what works for you, your life, and your body.

CHAPTER 3

BELIEFS

IF VICTORIAN
DOCTORS COULD
BELIEVE THAT
SOME PEOPLE
HAD GHOSTS
IN THEIR BLOOD
OR WHATEVER,
YOU CAN PROBABLY
BELIEVE IN YOURSELF
A LITTLE BIT.

BELIEVING IN YOURSELF

Whatever religious or spiritual beliefs you may or may not have about the wider world, I want to start by talking about believing in yourself.

<u>Do you believe you exist?</u> Hopefully you do. (Although saying that, I do frequently indulge in a little existential crisis to keep my feet on the ground.) The type of self-belief I'm actually talking about here is a little bit more complicated than that. I'm talking about believing in your infinite capacity to be wonderful, make good decisions, change things, learn new skills, and do hard things.

Easier said than done, I know. So when the self-doubt kicks in and I need to rediscover my self-belief, I use this one easy trick you won't believe…

I MAKE A SHORT LIST OF **THINGS I'VE DONE** THAT I PREVIOUSLY NEVER BELIEVED I WOULD EVER BE ABLE TO DO.

WHAT'S ON YOUR LIST?

LIMITING BELIEFS

So despite all the things we **know** we can do, we still tend to create beliefs about ourselves, the world around us, and what is possible for us that don't do us an awful lot of good. They are called limiting beliefs, and they are spectacularly unhelpful. Limiting beliefs are things, usually about ourselves or our potential, that we have come to accept in our minds as the truth.

They can be things like:

- I AM NOT CREATIVE
- I AM NOT GOOD WITH MONEY

- I AM UNLOVABLE
- I AM NOT GOOD ENOUGH

What a buzzkill, right?

We probably all have at least one or two limiting beliefs that are holding us back.

For this next activity, try to think of yourself as a lovely little caterpillar. You're currently wrapped up in your limiting beliefs like a cocoon. You need to break out of those thoughts and become the wonderful butterfly you were born to be!

YOU

YOUR LIMITING BELIEFS

IF YOU CAN BREAK FREE FROM YOUR LITTLE COCOON AND OVERCOME THEM

THEY FORM A PROTECTIVE SHIELD TO KEEP YOU SAFE (BUT A BIT STUCK)

YOU GET TO BE A BUTTERFLY - STILL YOU, BUT WITH BIG OL' FANCY WINGS YOU CAN USE TO GO WHEREVER YOU WANT TO GO!

Think about what limiting belief you want to work on. If you're struggling to decide, think about something you really want to do but seem to have a mysterious resistance to. That's a great shadowy hiding place for your limiting beliefs.

I THINK...

Find evidence to challenge that belief. You don't need to prove you are an artistic genius to show you are creative. But maybe you've found a creative solution to a problem, or you've got a good eye for color, or you can do cute bubble writing and have plans to make a career out of doing that...

BUT...

Separate yourself from the belief. When the thought comes up, notice it, remember your evidence, and let it pass right out of your brain. Eventually, you can separate yourself from something that once felt integral to your existence, just like the butterfly and its cocoon. What amazing thing will you do now?

I WILL...

REMEMBER: THIS IS ONE OF THOSE VERY HARD THINGS. LIMITING BELIEFS ARE A BIG DEAL.

TAKING COMFORT IN SOMETHING THAT ISN'T YOUR PAJAMAS

As well as having total, unflinching belief in yourself (or at least getting there slowly), there are thousands of other things you might also believe in that can bring contentment and joy to your life. Whether it is an organized religion, a connection to the magic of the universe, or just the opinion that everything happens for a reason, these bigger beliefs can be a real source of comfort in difficult times and give us the confidence to overcome new challenges.

When your beliefs bring you happiness and strength, it can be easy to think you should try and get other people to believe the same thing. But, inevitably, not everyone is going to think the same way as you. If we all believed in the same thing, it might be nice, or it might be terrible—I don't know, but it's never going to happen.

It's like when I got a new mattress and I went around telling everyone who would listen about my mattress and why they should also get the same mattress. I know, deep down in my heart, that I am **absolutely 100% correct** that my mattress would improve their lives.

But most people already have their own mattresses. Some people aren't satisfied with what they have, so they might give mine a go and join my exceptional mattress movement. Other people are okay with what they have now and can't be bothered to go about the hassle and expense of trying something new when it might not be that much better (even though it **definitely would be**). And finally, some people already have their own dream mattresses that they truly believe to be the best mattress in the world.

Sure, I could drag those people into my bed and make them lie down and awkwardly stare at them and demand that they agree I was right all along, but really, we're getting a bit carried away now I think.

I THINK IT'S PRETTY CLEAR THAT I'M THE BEST MATTRESS, BUT IF YOU'RE UNDECIDED, I'M NOT GOING TO PRESSURE YOU IF YOU NEED TO SLEEP ON IT.

And that's the point about beliefs—if you believe in something strongly enough, it's easy to start thinking you've got it all figured out and everyone else is wrong. That's fine. It is important to have conviction in yourself and your beliefs. The hard work can be accepting that other people might also feel the same about their completely opposite beliefs. Let everyone enjoy what they enjoy, believe what they believe, and sleep on their potentially inferior mattresses. It's the right thing to do and you'll still get a good night's sleep.

ZZZ

IF YOU'VE BEEN
WAITING FOR

A
POSITIVE
SIGN

THIS IS IT!

EVERYTHING HAPPENS FOR A REASON

It's undeniable that life always has a way of surprising you.

No matter how detailed your plans, at some point, they will be derailed. When they do, it **might** feel like a wonderful opportunity to change things in a way you had never considered, but, realistically, it will probably feel stressful, unfair, or miserable—at least at first.

Whenever this happens to me, and it does, seemingly quite often at the moment, I don't rush into trying to make myself feel better. That never helps. But what I do is try to remember, even when I'm feeling pretty terrible, that up until this point, things have all turned out to be vaguely okay.

All the things that have completely thrown me off, tested me, and even broken my heart have taught me something or pushed my life toward where I am now. And, as I'm relatively happy right now, ergo, all of those things, while they might not have been positive overall, have had at least some good come from them in the end.

So, when you get knocked off course, feel those feelings, but maybe see if you can find some comfort knowing that everything up until this point has probably just about turned out okay eventually, and there is no reason why that trend shouldn't continue.

IF IT'S MEANT TO BE, IT WILL HAPPEN...

BUT NOT MAGICALLY, WITHOUT ANY INVOLVEMENT FROM YOU.

IF IT'S MEANT TO BE, IT WILL HAPPEN

BECAUSE YOU'VE PUT YOUR HEART AND SOUL INTO IT AND

MADE IT HAPPEN

ONE WAY OR ANOTHER.

MAGIC + MANIFESTATION

Whether you are sitting in a room surrounded by crystals or you are the sort of person who rolls their eyes when someone tells you their moon sign, I think it's nice to think that there is some kind of magic somewhere in our lives.

If you've been on the internet in the last 10 years, I'm going to assume you've heard about a type of magic called manifestation. Back in the day, I read a tween magazine that described this type of "cosmic ordering," and I thought it sounded brilliant. All I have to do is ask the universe for some platform shoes so I can be a Spice Girl and they will just turn up? Perfect.

Unfortunately, it wasn't quite that simple. Manifestation is a type of magic that only really works if you believe in it. And the magic part of that is actually **you**. You make things happen because you have committed to believing that you can make them happen, and so you put your heart and soul into it. It's like the opposite of a limiting belief and more like a wonderful self-fulfilling prophecy.

Does that make it any less magic? No. I don't think so.

So next time you are facing something difficult, I can't promise a fairy godmother will appear with a magical solution. But if you can manage unhelpful limiting beliefs and channel the good ones, you might be surprised by the powerful, important magic inside yourself. Believe in that.

A LITTLE REMINDER:

YOU ARE MAGICAL AS HECK

TODAY IS GOING TO BE GREAT.

BECAUSE OF THE MOON,
OR CRYSTALS, OR SOMETHING
LIKE THAT.

WHATEVER, IT'S GOING TO BE GREAT!

CHAPTER 4
DIRECTION

OFTEN I THINK ABOUT SOMEONE ELSE "GOSH, THEY'VE REALLY GOT IT TOGETHER, I WISH I WAS MORE LIKE THEM." AND THEN I WONDER IF ANYONE THINKS LIKE THAT ABOUT ME, AND THEN I JUST laugh + laugh for hours + hours AT THE RIDICULOUSNESS OF IT ALL, AND THINK WELL I MIGHT AS WELL JUST CRACK ON.

WHEN YOU GROW UP...

Life felt like it had a bit more direction when I was young. I was definitely going to be a hairdresser, like my auntie. That was basically the whole plan, and that was probably the last time I ever felt certain I knew what was going to happen next in life.

But I didn't become a hairdresser. I still can't even blow-dry my own hair properly, so it seems unlikely I'm ever going to tick that particular item off my to-do list. And that's fine. Sure, if I told five-year-old Veronica this, she might be a bit upset, but the idea of me learning hairdressing now fills me with absolute, utter ~~dread~~ neutrality. (See, I can't even summon dread. Hairdressing means basically nothing to me now.)

The point of this story is **not** to highlight my failures or insult hairdressers, but rather to say that sometimes you start your journey heading in one direction and end up taking a completely different path. So while you might have a wistful moment when you think back to your childhood dreams of becoming a pilot, a veterinarian, or Ultimate Ruler of the Universe, there's a reason you took a different path. And who knows, maybe you're still on your way there and you don't even realize it yet.

STAY EXCITED

ABOUT THE *possibilities*

AND STAY OPEN

TO THE *possibilities* YOU

HAVEN'T *even considered*

KEEPING AN OPEN MIND

Staying open-minded about where you are heading and what you are doing with your life, or your weekend, or the next hour, can result in the most magical outcomes. There are definitely times where it's great to stay focused on your ultimate goal and not let anything deter you from getting there. But life also has a way of waiting until you think you have absolutely 100% set your mind to something before sneakily showing you a totally different option you hadn't even thought about and a clear and obvious path to get there.

So how do you know when you should stick with the plan and when you should mix it up? Well, that's a tricky one. There is nothing inherently wrong with either option—some people love a plan and do what they set out to do every single time. Other people go with the flow by default. Life means that often we have to be **flexible** and exist somewhere between the two. As a general rule, when the route you are currently on seems too long, too treacherous, or is taking you to places you have no interest in visiting, it is probably time to take out your map and start recalculating.

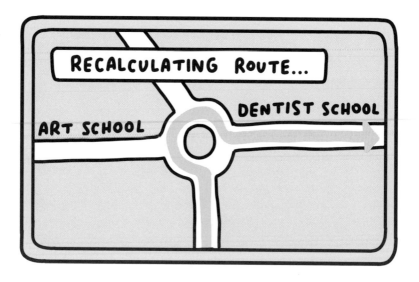

DON'T WORRY ABOUT PEOPLE OVERTAKING YOU. WE'RE ALL GOING TO DIFFERENT PLACES.

THANK GOODNESS, OTHERWISE THERE WOULD PROBABLY BE NOWHERE TO SIT WHEN YOU ARRIVE + THAT WOULD BE REALLY RUBBISH + ANNOYING.

THINGS THAT ARE TRUE

IT'S OKAY TO FEEL A BIT SAD IF YOU SEE SOMEONE DOING SOMETHING YOU WANTED TO DO BUT HAVEN'T GOT AROUND TO YET.

IT DOESN'T MEAN THAT THEY ARE A BAD PERSON OR HAVE "SOLD OUT."

IF THAT THING WAS A PRIORITY FOR YOU RIGHT NOW, YOU MIGHT HAVE DONE IT TOO. WE ALL HAVE DIFFERENT PRIORITIES AT DIFFERENT TIMES OF OUR LIVES AND THAT'S FINE.

As we've already touched upon, comparing yourself to other people and what they're doing is a **sure-fire way** to make you feel bad about yourself. Chances are, at some point in your life, you've watched someone you know go after the same things you wanted and got them. That can sting. It's okay to be a bit jealous. But it's also not okay to decide they are somehow a bad person because they went and did the thing you wanted to do. Unless that thing is like, cutting down the rainforest or something. But you shouldn't want to do that either.

JUST BECAUSE
YOU DON'T KNOW
HOW TO DO IT
YET DOESN'T
MEAN YOU CAN'T
DO IT.

FEELING LOST (AND HOW TO FIND YOUR WAY)

Sometimes, it's not even that you start heading in one direction but get lured in by a different path. Sometimes, you can't even see the next step in front of you, and that can absolutely be the hardest place to be. Maybe you just have absolutely no idea what you want to do with your life. Or your life has gone in an unexpected direction that now feels more like a dead end.

Read through these questions, see which one stands out to you, and then write about it on the next page:

☺ Do you need to spend more time in the exact spot you're in right now? Is it a moment of pause that you need whilst you gather your thoughts? (A moment can mean anything from a few hours to a few months.)

♥ Is there something in your past that is calling you back?

☺ Is there somewhere else you feel like you were supposed to be right now? Maybe you need to accept you will never make it there before you can move on, or maybe you need to make a new plan on how to get there.

♥ What feels like happiness for you right now? Where do you imagine yourself? How can you get to that place?

☺ Is there an obstacle that's stopping you from getting anywhere at all? Maybe tackling that obstacle is the only direction you need right now. Once you climb that mountain, you'll have a better view of what's ahead of you.

I FEEL LOST BECAUSE...

LIFE IS THE JOURNEY
DEATH IS THE DESTINATION

Is that too dark? Probably.

The point is that every single second of time we spend on learning something new, going to new places, or generally doing whatever we need to do to get to the next phase of our lives is, in fact, also a part of our life. So it's just as important to enjoy those bits (or at least try to) as it is the future when we get there. Otherwise, really, **what's the point of it all?**

For example, I'm all for earning enough money to spend my twilight years roaming around a plush retirement home making trouble, but that also seems like a distant dream. So while I'm happy to put the work in and put some money aside for my future happiness as I go (in theory… not going to pretend I've actually sorted my pension out yet), I'd quite like to spend most of the days leading up to that point in relative happiness, not just eating beans on toast and putting aside every last penny. Because:

#1 I LIKE TO BE HAPPY
☺ AND ENJOY AS MUCH OF MY TIME
AS POSSIBLE - WHO DOESN'T?

#2 I MIGHT NOT EVEN
☠ MAKE IT TO THAT PARTICULAR
DESTINATION

I literally might die before I get to the retirement home. I could spend my whole life scrimping and saving and not even get to retirement age. In which scenario, I will refer back to, **what's the point of it all?**

While I'm not suggesting you spend all your old-person-retirement-home-weird-creepy-ornament fund on gadgets that the internet keeps advertising to you to help you curl your hair overnight or whatever, I am saying you've got to strike a balance.

Whether the direction you are heading in right now involves sacrificing your time, your money, your mental capacity to deal with bullshit, or anything else, just consider the balance. Your destination will undoubtedly be worth some sacrifices, but don't sacrifice your entire present for a future that might not actually arrive.

And on that (slightly morbid) note, let's think about something nice for a minute, like fluffy dogs with stripy pajamas on. Phew.

CHAPTER 5

CHANGE

IF YOU CAN REDEFINE YOUR EYEBROWS EVERY MORNING, YOU CAN DEFINITELY REDEFINE YOURSELF ANY TIME YOU WANT TO.

CHANGE IS GOOD

IT'S ALSO SCARY. BUT SOMETIMES SCARY IS GOOD. LIKE ROLLERCOASTERS AND CUTE GHOSTS. NOT HORROR FILM TYPE GHOSTS THOUGH.

I'm not much of a person for changing something just for the sake of changing something, but I'm also not much of a person for keeping something the same just because that's how it's always been.

There is usually something in our lives, **big or small**, that we could change in the pursuit of life being a tiny bit better in some way. I try to keep myself committed to finding those things and changing them.

CHANGE CAN BE A LOT OF THINGS, SOMETIMES ALL AT ONCE:

SCARY BIG SMALL WORTH IT EASY OVERWHELMING A MISTAKE* HARD MAGICAL

*BUT THAT DOESN'T NECESSARILY MEAN THAT YOU SHOULDN'T TRY IT.

Usually, the reason we resist change is just because we know that things are fine as they are. Or, at least, they haven't resulted in our untimely death or the downfall of civilization. That resistance to change is just you trying to keep yourself in your comfort zone. But what if I told you that there is some seriously cool shit just outside your comfort zone?

Well, there is. And usually you have to make a few changes to get to the coolest shit. That's just how it works.

YOU'VE CHANGED

IT IS WHAT IT IS, BUT IT HASN'T ALWAYS BEEN

Things **right now**, right at this very moment, are exactly what they are. But they haven't always been that way. It's easy to think that nothing has changed, when in reality, you've probably been constantly making changes for most of your life, just maybe not realizing how extremely proactive you have been already.

Let's play a quick round of "look at how far you've come" to see the wonderful things that have already changed. Choose a few different points in your life and look at what changed to get you to the next part. It could be changes to relationships, career, or location.

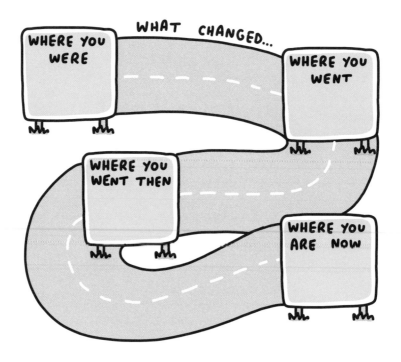

Fun, right? So accomplished! Such a change maker!

Next up, think about somewhere you'd like to go (now we've got **direction** all covered) and think about the changes that would need to happen for you to get well on your way there ...

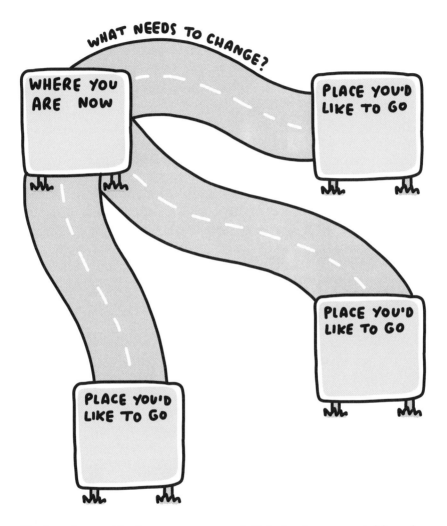

WHAT NEEDS TO CHANGE?

WHERE YOU ARE NOW

PLACE YOU'D LIKE TO GO

PLACE YOU'D LIKE TO GO

PLACE YOU'D LIKE TO GO

You've changed before, so you can definitely change again! Let the petrifying fear wash over you, and then enjoy the tingly, exciting sense of anticipation coming to the front of your awareness, and ride that wave of sensation all the way to the place (or places) you're heading.

NO SHAME IN CHANGING YOUR MIND. AND CHANGING IT AGAIN.

I don't think we're really designed to stay still for too long. Life isn't about making a finite number of changes to get things **just right** and then existing in that one particular way forever.

SOMETIMES, YOU'LL MAKE A CHANGE AND WANT TO CHANGE BACK.

SOMETIMES, YOU'LL MAKE A CHANGE AND WANT TO CHANGE IT EVEN MORE.

SOMETIMES, YOU'LL MAKE A CHANGE AND WANT TO CHANGE IT AGAIN COMPLETELY IN A WHOLE NEW WAY.

NONE OF THESE THINGS MEAN THAT YOU SHOULDN'T HAVE CHANGED ANYTHING IN THE FIRST PLACE.

There is **absolutely no shame** in changing your mind. There is no shame in finding out that actually the thing you thought you wanted isn't right for you. There is no shame in trying new things, reinventing yourself, or starting again, over and over, if that's what feels like the right thing for you.

YOU ARE NOT TOO OLD AND IT IS NOT TOO LATE.*

* OBVIOUSLY, IF IT'S 9PM, IT IS TOO LATE TODAY, BUT THERE'S STILL TOMORROW

WHEN ARE YOU GOING TO SETTLE DOWN?

The world has changed and, with it, the idea that we will follow the same template for life that seemed to be pretty universal 50 years ago. People might have expectations of your life that just don't suit you. Sometimes it is things they think you **should** be doing, sometimes it is things you **shouldn't** be doing. And that's why when you announce that, aged 45, you are going to retrain as a Monkey Rescue Ranger, Grandma might roll her eyes and mutter about you never being able to stick with anything.

NOW, YOUR GRANDMA IS PROBABLY JUST...

TRYING TO KEEP YOU SAFE

Staying in your current job as a Grade 34 Bureaucrat certainly makes more sense on paper, because you are already doing it and therefore it is a safe option. Grandma doesn't know how much a Monkey Rescue Ranger earns or how steady a job it is, so naturally, she's going to be a little nervous on your behalf.

A LITTLE BIT JEALOUS

Because perhaps Grandma never had the chance to throw caution to the wind and follow her dreams, and who wouldn't be jealous of a Monkey Rescue Ranger?

Once you get past your own resistance to making a big change, you will find a long line of other people showing up to register their concerns. Great, thanks so much for coming. Now, you probably won't want to listen to everyone, but it's likely that there are some people you will feel obligated to allow at least a little bit of input into your decision-making processes.

Here are some ideas on how to handle that advice with good grace…

A LIST OF THINGS YOU MIGHT WANT TO DO WHEN PEOPLE GET UP IN YOUR BUSINESS…

ASSUME POSITIVE INTENT

BE GRATEFUL THAT THEY CARE ENOUGH TO BE WORRIED

CHANGE YOUR MIND

DECIDE WHETHER YOU SHARE THEIR WORRY AND DEAL WITH IT

REASSURE THEM

IGNORE THEM

DO IT ANYWAY

THE ALTERNATIVE TO CHANGE
IS STAYING THE SAME...

It's easy to get stuck. I feel like the further you go through life, or the longer you put up with something that isn't right, the harder it is to change it later on.

Let's just jump in the deep end and use marriage as an example. A wonderful friend of mine recently told me that she is getting a divorce. She then went on to tell me how disappointed she is that everyone who she told before me said "I'm so sorry!", when she saw it as a huge positive and opportunity to move on and change her life for the better.

Of course, such a change did involve some sadness and is likely to involve a certain amount of uncertainty and stress. But a divorce is so much more than an ending. It's a **new start**, too.

Consider what constant in your life you are married to, metaphorically. It could be your job, a hobby, or a pair of worn, tatty jeans.

 Do you want to stay married because it's easier, even though you know you would be much happier apart?

Are you celebrating each anniversary as an achievement, even if finishing things would actually be a much more valuable achievement for you?

Have you given so many years to this marriage that starting over again hardly seems worth all the fuss, even though the years to come represent opportunities for a fresh start?

Only you can decide whether a difficult change will be worth it. You know the one I mean—your gut is telling you already. And my gut is telling me to tell you that you have one precious life and I'd really like it if you did make some big decisions and do some hard things in the pursuit of your ultimate happiness.

And I'll leave you with one last tip for when you make that big change. There are lots of people in the world who hope to influence you. There are people who will profit from your failures, as well as people who will profit from your successes. There are people who will cheer you on regardless. However hard these people try and give you advice from the back seat, remember…

YOU ARE IN THE DRIVING SEAT

THERE IS
ONE PERSON
WHO *needs to be happy*
WITH ANY CHANGES
YOU MAKE

THERE IS
ONE PERSON
WHO CAN *choose* HOW
THEY RESPOND TO CHANGES
THEY MIGHT NOT HAVE
CONTROL OVER

THERE IS
ONE PERSON
THAT *you* ARE *accountable*
TO AND WHO CAN *motivate*
YOU TO *change* THINGS

**SURPRISE! THAT
PERSON IS YOU!**

CHAPTER 6

FAMILY

BLOOD IS THICKER THAN WATER, BUT NOT AS THICK AS CUSTARD. CUSTARD IS SWEET, LIKE LOVE, AND LOVE IS ALL THAT MATTERS.

ONCE UPON A TIME

Wouldn't it be lovely if we all lived in a fairytale? (If we ignore all the bad stuff that seems to happen in most fairytales that is, and just take the "happily ever after" bit.) We'd all be in our own little royal family, living in a castle, wearing tastefully coordinating outfits, eating banquets together, with magic and treasure and other fun stuff, and this chapter would probably be quite easy to write.

Unfortunately, and I suspect you've noticed this already, but just in case: we don't live in a fairytale. In **real life**, families come in many different forms and have very different stories.

There are the families we're born into. There are the "in-law" families we become bonded to because we fell in love with one of their members. Families might change or expand further because someone else falls in love and creates a new, merged family. You might feel like you are a part of many different families. Your close friends or even your colleagues may feel more like siblings than those you share genetic material with. Maybe you live in a tight-knit community and feel like your neighbor is more of a mother to you than the person who gave birth to you. Maybe you grew up in a forest and have a family of wolves, although I suspect that we might be verging on fairytale territory again with that one...

The similarity all these families have is that they come from a place of good old-fashioned love. Also, although you love them, you might not always get along with them. Family is **complicated**. Sorry about that.

THERE'S MORE THAN ONE TYPE OF TREE

Perhaps your family tree looks like a perfectly symmetrical oak tree, with all the people in traditional places, going back generation after generation. If you can't fit your family tree into that diagram though, don't worry. There's plenty of other types of trees in the woods. My family tree isn't too wild, but it is a bit like those classic cartoon trees that grew too close to each other and got all twisted together and a few branches fell off, but hey, what a visual.

How do you imagine your family tree?

GROWING YOUR FAMILY

While people generally seem to be moving slowly away from the classic milestones of "fall in love… get married… have 2.4 children," they are still very much an expectation for a lot of people. That expectation can be annoying when other people push it on you, but can also leave you putting pressure on yourself.

Growing or adding to your family is a big decision. Whether your idea of adding to your family is spending your life savings on fertility treatment for a much-wanted baby, or deciding that children aren't for you and you want to get a dog instead, it's a **big deal**, and neither option is a less valid life choice.

As both a dog owner and a parent of human children, I could sit here and make a bullet-point list of all the reasons you should make the same decision as me because "Woo! I'm so happy." But when I think about it logically, there are also times I could make equally long lists about how hard it is and alternatives you could choose that could make you happier because they suit you better.

ULTIMATELY, THESE ARE DECISIONS YOU NEED TO MAKE BASED ON YOU, YOUR LIFE, AND WHAT YOU WANT FROM IT.

So that's all I'm going to say on this massive topic. After all, the last thing you want is to feel like these decisions have been made for you (or are being dictated to you by a book that promised it would make your life a little bit easier and not give you a hard time).

IT'S NOT ALWAYS EASY

Whatever form your family takes, one of the reasons we might surround ourselves with family, blood relatives or otherwise, is because it is (or can be) mutually beneficial. We can provide each other with love, care, and support, in many different forms.

However, family relationships, while they can be incredibly rewarding, can be some of the most complicated relationships we have to navigate...

♡ There are often family relationships that require us to deal with things that we wouldn't usually tolerate from other people. If you are a parent, looking after your child will require sacrifices and hard work often in the face of completely unreasonable behavior.

🌈 You might feel an incredibly strong bond with a family member that requires you to make compromises you wouldn't make for anyone else in the world.

☺ The boundaries we set within our wider lives can become very blurred when it comes to our families, and even if they are still the same, your family might consider them to be more flexible or just generally push them to the limit.

And this isn't to say that you have to automatically accept anything they throw at you—you absolutely don't—it's just an acknowledgment that it can be really bloody hard sometimes.

I KNOW FAMILIES CAN BE HARD. BUT HEY, AT LEAST YOURS PROBABLY WON'T EAT YOU.

YOU CAN'T KEEP EVERYONE HAPPY ALL OF THE TIME...

BUT YOU _CAN_ MAKE YOURSELF _utterly_ MISERABLE TRYING, AND THAT'S WORKING OUT REALLY WELL FOR ME SO FAR.

BOUNDARIES

THEY'RE NOT JUST A BUZZWORD. BOUNDARIES ARE BLOODY BRILLIANT

Unless you are going to cut yourself off from the rest of the world and live in a cave, or a little boat, or on the moon, or something (absolutely no judgment by the way—you do your thing), you and your happiness will probably be affected in some way by your relationships with other people.

Boundaries are the best way to keep relationships peachy and minimize any misery that might otherwise result. Setting and maintaining healthy boundaries can make you feel better, not just because they help to prevent something you don't like from happening, but also because you have taken control of the situation. Personally, making this sort of proactive move always gives me a little boost of confidence and self-esteem. I hope it does for you, too!

👀 SETTING BOUNDARIES CAN LOOK LIKE... 👀

♡ Reminding your sister not to comment on your appearance.

☺ Telling your partner that you need a couple of hours a week alone without them or your children.

♡ Asking that your neighbor doesn't pop round without making a prior arrangement.

☺ Insisting that the people you share your home with knock before coming into your room.

🧠 DECIDING YOUR BOUNDARIES 🧠

Think about things you find challenging to deal with, and spend some time thinking about ways you can make them easier for yourself, and protect your energy and mental well-being.

What feels right? What will work for you and your life? There's no rush, and you don't need to come up with a whole list. If one thing is bothering you, one boundary will be a great start.

_____

_____

_____

_____

_____

_____

⦿ COMMUNICATING YOUR BOUNDARIES ⦿

This might be the trickiest part, because the idea of it can feel a bit confrontational.

First, be clear to yourself why you need to put this boundary in place, so you're not tempted to back down.

Use "I' statements where possible, such as "I feel very defensive when you comment on my appearance, because I'm already a bit self-conscious and it feels a bit hurtful and critical. I need you to just be mindful of that and not mention it anymore."

Own it. It's not necessarily going to be an easy conversation, but you're doing it to protect and improve not just yourself, but also the relationship. So while the other person might feel momentarily defensive, it's the best for both of you in the long run.

Rehearse what you are going to say. Write it down here, if you want.

_____

_____

_____

_____

_____

_____

_____

THE ART OF COMPROMISE

Learning to compromise effectively can make life and all the relationships within it feel a lot easier. Sure, it would be wonderful if you could get your way all the time, but… actually, would it though? Or would you just turn into a monster? I think I would.

COMPROMISE ISN'T ALWAYS ABOUT MEETING IN THE MIDDLE

Sure, sometimes it will be. And sometimes it will be that you get your way. Other times, the other person might get their way, and other times, more often than not, it's finding an entirely new way that might not be perfect for either of you but actually satisfies everyone's needs.

It's all about being a bit flexible. But not so flexible that you snap.

Maybe you'll have to bend a boundary on this occasion as a sacrifice to the greater good (the effectiveness of the relationship), but that doesn't mean you should next time.

WHEN IT COMES TO COMPROMISE, BE LIKE A SWISS ROLL

… roll with it, and bend just enough to make a delightful treat, and not so much that you're just a soggy broken (probably angry) cake.

No one wants that. I'd still eat it, but I wouldn't want to.

ULTIMATELY, WHEN IT COMES TO FAMILY, IT'S OKAY IF...

YOUR FAMILY IS NOT "conventional"

THERE'S more than ONE GROUP OF PEOPLE YOU'D CONSIDER FAMILY

YOU NEED TO SET boundaries

YOU NEED TO protect YOUR ENERGY + EMOTIONS AND PUT yourself FIRST SOMETIMES

THE DYNAMICS WITHIN YOUR FAMILY change OVER TIME

YOU HAVE TO MAKE compromises SOMETIMES

THINGS DON'T WORK OUT.

CHAPTER 7
FRIENDS
(AND OTHER PEOPLE)

☺

SO NO ONE TOLD YOU LIFE WAS GOING TO BE THIS WAY...

FULL OF PEOPLE AND THEIR WAYS.

FRIENDS ARE THE FAMILY YOU CHOOSE YOURSELF

But, I mean, we've already kind of covered family in the last chapter and how your friends can actually be your family. So rather than repeating myself, this chapter will be about friends, but also people in general.

Having good people in your life can make the world seem a little bit easier to deal with. Whether you have one or two close friends. Or you have a million friends (but most of them live in your computer). Or you're one of those people who has stayed friends with a big group from middle school, or even college, and you still do everything together (I'm always a bit jealous of those ones). Basically, whatever your friendship vibe is, nurturing those relationships is worthwhile and important.

But, while that is true and lovely, if you're reading this and thinking "**<u>Argh</u>** I am an adult and I want to make friends but I don't know how to," then it doesn't help much. That's why you need to turn over the page.

IF YOU WERE A FLOWER, I'D ~~PICK YOU~~
WANT TO BE A FLOWER NEARBY, SO WE
COULD HANG OUT A LOT + GROW TOGETHER.

HOW TO MAKE FRIENDS AS A GROWN UP

Making friends as a grown-up can be an overwhelming endeavor, but hey, we're here to learn how to do hard things...

FRIENDLINESS LEADS TO FRIENDSHIP

Be friendly! Know how sometimes you feel mega awkward and alone and you just wish someone would smile at you and say hi? Be that person for someone else.

PUT YOURSELF OUT THERE

Whether it's texting someone you haven't seen for a while for a catch up, or asking another parent in the schoolyard if they want to meet for a coffee at the park next week, make sure you are officially open to other people.

IT'S NOT WHAT YOU KNOW, IT'S WHO YOU KNOW

Give yourself a head start by building deeper relationships with people who are already acquaintances. Alternatively, ask a good friend to introduce you to their colleague or neighbor if they think you'd get on.

DO THINGS YOU LOVE DOING

We tend to connect best with people who love doing the same things as us (unless your thing is solo long-distance sailing trips or something similarly solitary). Once you discover you've got one thing in common, chances are you'll find more.

PRETEND FEAR OF REJECTION ISN'T A THING SOMEHOW

That one is easier said than done, I suppose. More on that next.

HAPPINESS IS NOT CARING WHAT OTHER PEOPLE THINK OF YOU.

SO EASY, RIGHT?

JUST DO THAT.

HOW TO CARE A tiny bit OTHER PEOPLE

The more you love yourself, the less you'll feel affected by other people's opinions of you. It's not as simple as waving a magic wand and falling in love with yourself. It takes work. Learning to accept the things about yourself that you may feel self-conscious about is a brilliant starting point.

Think about how much you actually notice of other people and how much more you tend to be

PERSPECTIVE

focused on what you are doing. Most of us are thinking like this and not, in fact, analyzing other people's every move. Next time you trip over, remember it is much more memorable for you than for anyone else that might have seen it happen. Take heart in that!

Surround yourself, wherever possible, with people who you feel comfortable with and can really be yourself around. The more you do, the more you begin to see the best in people and assume that bit of comfort with more people. And even if those people don't appreciate you in the end, at least you managed to stay true to you.

LESS ABOUT WHAT THINK ABOUT YOU...

MAKE THE SWITCH

We tend to be our own biggest critics. Make the switch to being your own best friend instead—talk to yourself with the same level of encouragement and generosity you would if you were having the same conversation with a BFF. Think about practical advice you might offer someone else. Be kind! We all need an inner BFF!

Realizing, and accepting, that we actually have very little control of the opinions others form of us can be quite freeing. Think of it like climate change, e.g., do the bits within your power and strive to be a good person, but don't let it keep you awake at night. A lot of it is out of your hands. People are influenced by so many external factors that you can never hope to control, and that's okay.

FOCUS ON WHAT YOU can CONTROL

I know THIS isn't THE POINT, BUT I THINK YOU'RE **UTTERLY BRILLIANT!**

IDENTIFYING + DEALING WITH TOXIC PEOPLE

A toxic person isn't all glowing and green like they would be in a comic, and usually they aren't even really 100% a toxic person. More often, some element of their behavior is toxic. It is those things they do that make you feel crap and, in turn, like you want to put yourself in the bin.

This type of behavior is hard to spot, because things often don't start out toxic. It develops **gradually and subtly**, and you might not always realize it is the cause of you feeling more and more crappy. A bit like the proverbial frog in water that is getting hotter so gradually that they don't notice they're being boiled alive (what a weird and disturbing proverb...).

So what should you be on the lookout for? Here are a few behaviors that can turn a relationship toxic if repeated often or used in combination:

POSSIBLE SIGNS OF TOXICITY

DELIVERING UNHELPFUL CRITICISM

We can all benefit from someone who isn't afraid to give us honest and constructive criticism which can help guide us to something better. But if the criticism feels relentless and OTT, it's not the one.

SUPPLYING ENDLESS NEGATIVITY

We all have our reasons for being negative from time to time, especially if we have our own things going on. But if you're getting nothing but negativity from someone, it's a huge drain. Some people thrive on finding fault with everything, and there's only so much you can put up with that before it starts to drag you down to the same level, and you start to only see the bad in the world around you.

TAKING PLEASURE IN YOUR MISTAKES

Needs no explanation really—this is not cool, not cool at all. Being a bit jealous sometimes is natural, even with your loved ones, but there's a line that shouldn't be crossed.

HOLDING YOU BACK FOR THEIR BENEFIT

This might happen most often in a work environment, but not exclusively. People can react poorly when something changes in a hierarchy or social structure they are part of. It is often because they feel insecure and unsettled, but that's for them to deal with. It isn't an excuse for trying to hold you back, trip you up, or undermine your confidence.

DUMPING THEIR RESPONSIBILITIES ONTO YOU

This isn't just for people who are delegating work in your direction way, way too much, but also for friends taking advantage of you. The more you help, the more they expect you to do, until you find yourself doing the most ridiculous things for them, with little appreciation. If you know they'd drop everything and do the same for you, that's one thing. But if it's not a two-way street, it might be time to rethink the relationship.

PUTTING OBSTACLES FOR NO GOOD REASON

"Oh, you're going to do this? Well, what about that thing I've just done that will make it more difficult." Great. Just like the people who love to complain, there are people who love to make life just that little bit more difficult for people around them. When someone is throwing so many spanners into the works that you might as well be wearing a tool belt, it's time to take action.

LIFE'S TOO SHORT AND YOU'RE TOO AMAZING TO LET TOXIC PEOPLE BRING YOU DOWN

DETOXIFYING YOUR LIFE

YOU'VE IDENTIFIED A TOXIC PERSON, NOW WHAT?

✓ KNOW THE SIGNS

Once you're familiar with what toxic behavior looks like, you can be super vigilant. Recognize it as it happens, and it'll be easier to stop it from becoming a pattern. This one is easy, because we just learned some of the signs, so I've ticked it off for you right away!

☐ CHECK YOUR BOUNDARIES

As humans, we tend to have a different set of boundaries for each relationship we have. That's totally fine and normal; we tend to give more leeway to those closest to us. It's worth reexamining those boundaries periodically though. If you're feeling a bit vulnerable, take a look at what you expect from people vs. what you get and how that makes you feel. Communicate if things aren't working for you. This doesn't need to involve a big confrontation—a gentle text message or phone call can go a long way.

☐ NO DRAMA, NO, NO, NO DRAMA

A bit of drama in your life now and then is to be expected, but don't get pulled into it when it can be avoided. If there's someone in your life stirring up chaos (real or invented) and you find yourself right in the middle of it, then maybe you need to tell them you're finding it stressful, or distance yourself completely. Try to make your headspace more of a drama-free zone of calm.

DRAMA-FREE ZONE DRAMA-FREE ZONE

FOCUS ON THE GOOD SHIT

If you've got friends who try to pull toxic crap on you and friends who don't, the second lot should win every time. Spend time fostering the positive relationships.

DON'T WAIT FOR CHANGES

People don't change unless they want to. You can't fix them, you don't have to make excuses for them, you just have to take responsibility for your end of things.

IT TAKES TIME

If you cut someone out of your life, that's an instant fix. But most of the time, when you are just making small changes in a relationship, you probably won't see big results straight away. Don't let this frustrate you. Taking small, consistent action in reducing the amount of toxic behavior you tolerate day-to-day will have a huge positive effect in the long run.

Remember, above all else, if someone makes you feel bad for not wanting to put up with their bad behavior, you 100% shouldn't. You are awesome and will only ever get more awesome by prioritizing putting toxic people in the bin. Color in this statement and repeat it to yourself over and over as you do, to fix it in your mind.

I DESERVE TO BE FREE OF TOXIC INFLUENCES

SOME PEOPLE ARE
JUST THE WORST.
YOU CANNOT FIX
THEM, AND YOU
DON'T HAVE TO
MAKE EXCUSES
FOR THEM.

DON'T LET THEM DRAG YOU DOWN.

CHAPTER 8

LOVE

LOVE IS ALL
YOU NEED.
ALSO FOOD,
SHELTER, OXYGEN,
IDEALLY A STABLE
SOCIETY, SOLID
HEALTHCARE + A
BIT OF EDUCATION
MAYBE?

BUT MAINLY LOVE, LOVE AND
ALL THAT OTHER STUFF.

ALL YOU NEED IS LOVE
LIFE IS BETTER WITH LOVE IN IT.

Love is, in fact, all around. But if you only notice the sexy, romantic kind of love, then it might sometimes seem like it's in short supply. Having love in your life is about so much more than having a romantic partner. Of course, that might help, if that's what you're looking for, but there's a lot of love out there.

People you love. Things you love. Places you love.

WHERE IS THE LOVE?

Think about all the people, places, and things that make you feel love. Whether you love them or they love you… have a little love in. Right here, right now.

☺ PEOPLE ☺	♥ PLACES ♥

♥ OTHER THINGS ♥

YOU GIVE ME BUTTERFLIES

BUT I DON'T REALLY KNOW
WHAT TO DO WITH THEM.
IT'S KIND OF A WEIRD PRESENT.

LOVE IS A MANY SPLENDORED THING

Love isn't always easy, but it shouldn't always be difficult either. Sometimes (very, very, very rarely) you have to be cruel to be kind, but only in extreme circumstances, like when your partner starts saying things like "let's touch base on this" or "we'll put a pin in that and circle back later" and you have to tell them to piss off.

A good partnership should bring out the best in both of you. (Or all of you, if there's more than two. But two works for my next Spice Girls reference, so bear with me.)

"2 Become 1" is just a song. No matter how in love you are, you're still a person in your own right and deserve your own friends, hobbies, and time to yourself sometimes.

There will be challenges. Times when you question everything. Always ask those questions—don't hold the relationship to some impossible ideal that means you can't even check it is still happy and healthy.

There is no shame in getting help. In school, we learn about trigonometry and erosion, but the only way we really learn how to get along with each other in a healthy way is by watching other people (and movies). But if the people around us are just making it up as they go along, it's no surprise we tend to pick up bad habits. It isn't a failure to seek some more professional guidance.

Love doesn't always last forever, and don't let the idea that it should trick you into spending time making each other miserable.

YOU ARE THE AVERAGE OF THE 5 PEOPLE YOU SPEND MOST TIME WITH...

(PLUS THE 5 TV SERIES YOU REWATCH MOST FREQUENTLY.)

SO SURROUND YOURSELF WITH LOVE

We all express love in different ways. Some people call this having different "love languages."

Some of us are very soppy and open about our feelings. There is a reason shopping centers are full of those cheesy teddy bears holding little pun-filled notes. People literally buy them every day. See also, balloons. I guess maybe if you struggle to say your feelings out loud, then the little teddy can do a lot of heavy lifting with a "I love you beary much" sign...

Some of us are more likely to call the people we love an "absolute idiot" and show we care through (sometimes brutal) honesty and teasing. I guess the love is apparent by the fact you let each other get away with it, whereas a stranger saying the same things would be completely unacceptable.

Provided everyone involved understands and feels comfortable with how you're expressing your love, the actual method isn't really important. The important thing is that it's **happening**. So find your own love language and speak it often.

The more time you spend with love, the easier it becomes to love. Loving life, loving yourself, loving other people. Surround yourself with people you love, spend time in places you love being, and spend time doing the things you love doing. That's it—that's the tip.

YOU ABSO-LUTE IDIOT

PARENTAL
ADVISORY
CONTENT I FEEL
REALLY RATHER
AWKWARD ABOUT

IF YOU ARE READING THIS BOOK AND YOU'RE
RELATED TO ME IN ANY WAY, I REQUEST
THAT YOU SKIP THIS PART, AND TURN
DIRECTLY TO PAGE 96 OR AT LEAST
NEVER MENTION IT TO ME OUT LOUD.
THANK YOU IN ADVANCE.

REGULAR SEX

I like sex. In fact, **I love sex**. It's good.

There have been times in my adult life where I've had lots of intense, exciting, and liberating sex. Where I've felt like I'm in a dreamy haze of satisfaction and desire. There have also been times (mainly since getting the dog) where I have had basically zero sex. Sex is a big part of life for a lot of people, but not having regular sex does not necessarily mean you don't have a healthy and satisfying sex life.

I LIKE BEING IN YOUR BED

Just like everything else in life, we seem to follow cycles when it comes to sex. In my experience, the more I have sex, the more I want it. But then I get to a point where I think I need a bit of a rest and I'm happy to be left alone for the next few weeks and almost forget entirely what the fuss is about.

When it comes to how often you want to have sex, you probably know what works for you, and hopefully if you have a partner you can find a balance that keeps you both (or however many of you there are) on track for sexual happiness. That might involve a combination of sex together in the traditional sense and solo sex, because, while in a dream world you might have your needs satisfied by an expert team of sex gods/goddesses/mythical creatures of some sort, sometimes it's just easier to get yourself off.

And then there's the **other type** of regularity when it comes to sex, e.g., are you normal or are you a massive weirdo? But is there any such thing? Regularity I mean, not massive weirdos... I know there are massive weirdos because basically I am one. (Generally speaking, not sexually. Although, maybe sexually speaking too?)

I feel like these days we are reduced to, and divided into, two categories and pitted against each other. There are those who are happy having "vanilla" sex (whatever that even means... I guess ice cream is involved?). And then those who deviate from that are literally deviants. I mean, that's the definition of a deviant surely—someone who deviates? And the vanilla-sex people and the deviant-sex people are both equally perplexed as to how the other type can possibly be satisfied because it doesn't make any sense to them.

Whatever you find sexy, I'm fairly sure there is someone out there somewhere who's already made a website about it and dedicated their life to the practice of it, even if you feel like it's a bit... specialist.

Whether your desires come from some unchangeable internal sex compass, or they've grown on you over time, sharing them with a partner might feel like a scary thing to do. However, even if they aren't into something in the same way you are, there's usually something you can try together that you both feel comfortable with that will satisfy that curiosity in a **safe, consensual, and non-awkward** way.

And if it does feel a bit awkward to start that conversation, at least these days you can do it over text message. "By the way, I'm into dressing up like an ice queen and being thawed by red hot passion—do you fancy that?" No one even has to see that you are blushing as you send it.

I'M INTO
ROLE-PLAY.
ROLE-PLAYING AS
A MATURE, LIBERATED
PERSON WHO ISN'T
ASHAMED OR AFRAID
TO TALK ABOUT SEX.

I STILL MAYBE NEED A LITTLE BIT

OF PRACTICE THOUGH...

LET'S GET COMFORTABLE

Feeling comfortable is key when it comes to sex. Whether it's frequency, format, your choice of partner, or whether you even want to have it at all.

You need to trust that the person you're sharing your deepest desires and your body with is worthy of something so intimate. If you have that, everything else will follow. Enjoy! (Especially as the next chapter is about something much less enjoyable.)

OH HEY, I BOOKED US A CRUISE

VOYAGE OF SEXUAL DISCOVERY

SEE YOU AT THE HARBOR

CHAPTER 9

WORK

WORKING 9-5, IT'S NO WAY TO MAKE A LIVING.

BECAUSE THE KIDS DON'T GO INTO SCHOOL UNTIL 8:50AM AND I CAN'T TELEPORT YET FOR SOME REASON AND MY HUSBAND WORKS SHIFTS SO MOST OF THE TIME WE DON'T EVEN KNOW WHAT DAY IT IS. ALSO I'M MOST PRODUCTIVE FIRST THING IN THE MORNING AND COMPLETELY USELESS FROM AROUND 12-2, AND THEN AFTER THE 3:15 SCHOOL RUN THERE ARE APPROX 73 CLUBS EVERY WEEK ALL IN DIFFERENT PLACES WITH DIFFERENT UNIFORMS, AND THERE'S A HEALTHY DINNER TO BE COOKED. AND I WORK ON A COMPUTER AND HAVE THE INTERNET SO JUST WHY ON EARTH WOULD I EVEN TRY WORKING 9 TIL 5?

WORK-LIFE BALANCE

As more of us work from home, or read emails on our personal phones, or work on a side hustle at the weekend, the lines between work and life are blurring more than ever. But actually, what the heck does "work-life balance" mean anyway?

After all, we are still alive when we're at work, even if the job is soul-sucking or mind-numbing. So regardless of how hard you want to try to keep work in a neat little box, that box will contain a substantial portion of your time. So it is important that we like that part of life as much as we can.

Maybe you're reading this thinking "I hate my job but I can't just walk out because actual real life demands I pay bills and stuff like that, so the best thing is just to ignore it when I'm not there." Keeping work and life separate is your way of protecting yourself from letting that despair spill out into every other aspect of your life. I get it.

But we all want to be happy (I assume), so at some point—whether it's now, or sometime in the future when it's a bit easier to deal with—you're going to want to face up to the fact that you hate your job. The good news is I have some tips on what to do about it.

If you don't hate your job, great. Nailed it. Keep up the good work. You can skip to p.100.

DO WHAT YOU LOVE, LOVE WHAT YOU DO.

PAY YOUR BILLS
WITH GOOD VIBES.
IT'S ALL GOOD.

WHAT TO DO WHEN YOU HATE YOUR JOB

WORK OUT WHY YOU HATE IT

Is it the place you work, a horrible boss or annoying colleague, or is it your whole actual job?

MAKE A PLAN ACCORDINGLY

If you like your job but not your current employer, your plan might be to dust off your résumé and start applying for something new. If you are currently a builder and want to become a dentist, you should probably plan for some retraining before you start drilling into people's teeth.

SPREAD THAT PLAN OUT OVER HOWEVER LONG YOU NEED TO

Work out a reasonable time frame for each bit of your plan. Make it achievable, but also make sure it starts soon. Especially the first bit...

TAKE THE FIRST TINY STEP

This is crucial. Once you've taken the first step, even if it is as small as signing up to a newsletter with job alerts, the plan is officially in motion, and you're well on your way to a new work life.

WORK IT!

SO ANYWAY BACK TO THAT BALANCING ACT

You gotta do what you gotta do. I mean, that statement is vague to the point of being completely useless. But we all have very different needs when it comes to work-life balance, depending on what's going on in our career and our personal life.

Personally, I love working from home. I have no difficulty motivating myself even when wearing pajamas. While I do miss a bit of human contact, I don't miss it enough to justify working from an office or even going to "networking breakfasts" or anything potentially terrifying and awkward like that. But not everyone can work from home, either because their job doesn't allow it (I assume it is hard to be a sky-diving instructor from the sofa…) or because they just don't like it. Some people prefer having a daily routine that involves putting on a power suit, reading on the train, and sitting in an office full of colleagues, and all the social brilliance/drama that comes with that.

I'm also as happy as a clam to roll up my sleeves and power through busier days as and when they come. A late night here and there. Working a weekend to meet a big deadline. I thrive on an ebb and flow of work being busy and work being quiet. Perhaps some people prefer the predictability of set hours and days off which never change. The important thing is to find some sort of cycle that stops life becoming an endless grind. After all, if you're not careful, constant grinding will simply wear you away.

We also have to factor in our different needs. Our different living arrangements, demands on our income, our families, pets, hobbies, physical and mental capacity for working long hours, and what actually makes us happy. There're just **so many** variables.

So, ask yourself: What works for you? How can you get it?

MY DREAM WORK DAY

DAYS WORKED: ☁

HOURS WORKED: ☁

PLACE OF WORK (CIRCLE):

HOME   OFFICE   COFFEE SHOP   DESERT ISLAND

OTHER...

WORK WARDROBE (CIRCLE):

POWER DRESSING   LOUNGEWEAR   UNIFORM

FANCY DRESS   OTHER...

WORK TASKS:

LIFE TASKS:

NUMBER OF TEA BREAKS:

PERFECT LUNCH:

AFTER-WORK TREAT:

MAYBE SHE'S BORN WITH IT

MAYBE IT'S THAT SHE PUTS HER HEART AND SOUL INTO IT, NEVER STOPS WORKING, STAYS AWAKE ALL NIGHT WORRYING ABOUT PAYING THE BILLS AND NEVER REALLY FEELS LIKE SHE HAS HER SHIT TOGETHER BUT PRETENDS SHE DOES ANYWAY BECAUSE THAT'S WHAT PEOPLE DO.

SUCCESS AND HARD WORK

Success is a weird thing.

From the inside, you see all the hard work, bad bits, and probably don't really even notice the success, because you've already set your sights on the next task or goal. Whereas everyone on the outside only sees the good bits, so it can appear to them as if the success has just come out of nowhere. Basically, **the total opposite**.

It's why we look longingly at successful people and think it was so easy for them… they probably barely even did anything and just "landed on their feet"… how bloody annoying is their stupid face… etc. etc. etc. That's normal. But deep down, we're just protecting ourselves from the reality that they've got shit done that we'd like to do, and we're a bit jealous. (Luckily, there's already been a page about comparison, so I guess that is totally fixed and we don't have to worry about that bit.)

One of the other things that makes success so hard to define is that it's different for everyone, you included. It could be passing an exam, getting a promotion at work, saving up for a new sofa, or beating your personal best in the gym. You get to set your own vision for success, which is great. At least it is great until you forget what you were aiming for in the first place and start thinking that you aren't successful because you haven't got a big, detached house with a swimming pool or 50,000 bitcoins or whatever the person you're looking longingly at does have.

Basically, keep your eyes on your own prize. Focus on your stuff, acknowledge your hard work, and celebrate your successes, and that will probably make it maybe a tiny bit easier to be happy for strangers on the internet who look like they're doing really well.

BEING A PRODUCTIVE MEMBER OF SOCIETY

While I don't think we were just put on this planet to be productive at all costs (although don't ask me why we were actually put here, because I have no idea), I can appreciate that most of us want or need to get a certain amount of stuff done during the working day. And it's not always easy. In fact, for me, it rarely ever is. So here are my ultimate tips on getting stuff done:

Make a list. A detailed list. Put all the stuff you have to do on it, even showering. The adrenaline rush of checking something off will help carry you through to the next thing on the list.

Rest and take time off. If you don't rest, you'll just slow down to a barely productive state anyway, then beat yourself up about not getting much done, and then get even less done when you cry in your bed about what a failure you are. Rest is healthy **and** productive.

Ride your waves. We all have different times of day, week, and month when we are more or less effective. Work out what yours are and plan your hardest work for the right times. Leave mindless, repetitive tasks for the times you struggle to get your head in the game.

Be realistic. If you try to cram more into each day than you're actually capable of, you'll always feel like you're falling behind. Equally, if you only set yourself one or two short tasks, you'll either stretch them out and waste time, or you'll get bored and fed up.

THE EASIEST WAY TO GET SOMETHING DONE IS TO BLOODY WELL GET ON WITH IT.

CHAPTER 10
MONEY

MONEY CAN'T BUY YOU HAPPINESS.

BUT IT CAN BUY YOU PUPPIES, CRISPS, AND PAJAMAS SO I <u>DO</u> WANT SOME OF IT AND I'M NOT ASHAMED OF THAT.

LEARNING FROM NATURE: THE OSTRICH

When it comes to money, I've spent a lot of my life being a bit of an ostrich. You know, much angrier than you'd imagine and burying my head in the sand. (What a weird thing to do when you actually think about it literally?!) And if there's one other thing I know about ostriches other than the fact they do that, it's that none of them are rich. Not a single ostrich. So they are obviously not good role models when it comes to finances.

While searching the internet to confirm I was correct in my assumption that there are no rich ostriches, I actually learnt another thing about them—they are worth like $10k each. Wow. Why is that relevant here? Well, I think it helps me make a point... no matter how much you have struggled with or worried about money up to this point in your life, you are still extremely valuable and have untapped financial potential.*

So, first things first. If you find money a bit of a touchy subject, it's time to pull your head out of the sand.

*WITHOUT SELLING YOURSELF TO AN OSTRICH FARM. THERE'S AN EASIER WAY. PROBABLY.

WHAT'S THE WORST THING THAT COULD HAPPEN?

NO, I'M NOT BEING FLIPPANT, I MEAN LITERALLY WHAT IS THE WORST-CASE SCENARIO?

THE WORST-CASE SCENARIO

Okay, hopefully you aren't at rock bottom. But if you are, you know what they say: the only way is up. And when they say that, you're allowed to mentally punch them in the face because you're at rock bottom and that's the last thing you want to hear.

Being at rock bottom (or thinking about it) is scary, but I find the best way to tackle any issue is actually by thinking what the worst-case scenario could be and making a plan for that very situation. I figure, if I've got a plan for the absolute worst, then dealing with anything less terrible is going to be a breeze. This is a useful task, whatever your current financial situation is, so give it a try.

WHAT IS THE WORST THING THAT COULD HAPPEN RIGHT NOW AS A RESULT OF YOUR FINANCIAL SITUATION?

HOW COULD YOU DEAL WITH THAT?

YOU CAN MAKE
A FRESH START
AT ANY TIME,
EVEN AT 4PM
ON A THURSDAY.

TURN ME
OVER
WHENEVER
YOU LIKE IT

IT'S OFFICIALLY THE FIRST DAY OF THE REST OF YOUR LIFE

SO WHY NOT GIVE YOURSELF A LOVELY PRESENT?

Whatever has happened up to this point is in the past, and you can't do much about that. You might be dealing with the consequences right now, but basically, it is what it is, whether that's good or bad. So give Future You the gift of sorting your shit out once and for all.

BUDGETING, HUSTLING, SETTING UP AUTOMATIC SAVINGS, PUTTING TOGETHER A PLAN TO PAY OFF YOUR DEBTS, CUTTING YOUR BILLS, NOT BUYING AVOCADOS, SELLING YOUR OLD STUFF, OR BUYING CRYPTOCURRENCY.

Basically, there are like 50 million other books you can read about sorting out your finances and lots of different guidelines you can follow, but my one, critically important tip is that none of them will work unless you actually do the work. Whatever it is you need to do, actually doing it is the gift you're giving yourself. You are so generous. Future You is going to be so grateful!

MESSAGE FROM FUTURE YOU:

SERIOUSLY, CAN YOU JUST DEAL WITH THIS RIGHT NOW PLEASE SO I CAN JUST CHILL OUT FOR LIKE TWO SECONDS?

MONEY ISN'T A DIRTY WORD

Cash itself, totally different story—absolutely **filthy**. Wash your hands after you've touched any of that, completely revolting. Yuck. But the concept isn't necessarily something to feel shameful about. There are some common misconceptions about money, and if you believe them, it's going to really get in the way of dealing with your finances. Instead, remember:

TALKING ABOUT MONEY IS not VULGAR

WANTING MONEY BECAUSE IT WILL ALLEVIATE SOME OF YOUR WORRIES IS not GREEDY

WANTING MONEY SO THAT IT'S EASIER TO ENJOY YOUR LIFE IS also not GREEDY

ASKING FOR MORE MONEY IS NOT SOMETHING TO BE ashamed OF

Sure, it might be easier to tell yourself those classic lines to make it feel a bit more palatable when your bank balance isn't looking too healthy. I get it. But if you want to feel cool, calm, and in control of currency, it might be that you need to start reframing your thoughts about money.

QUESTION TIME

HOW DO YOU FEEL ABOUT MONEY NOW?

HOW DO YOU WANT TO FEEL ABOUT MONEY?

WHAT COULD HELP YOU GET THERE?

WHAT CAN MONEY DO FOR YOU?

NO REALLY, IN YOUR WILDEST DREAMS, WHAT COULD MONEY DO FOR YOU?

NOW, ASK YOURSELF
NOT WHAT MONEY CAN DO FOR YOU, BUT
WHAT CAN YOU DO FOR MONEY?

I think we have all fantasized about what we'd do if we have a bit (or a lot) more money. And if you haven't, you clearly didn't fill in the last activity, so go back and do that now... I'll wait.

It doesn't matter whether your ambition is just to feel more in control and have enough money to buy yourself a bunch of flowers every so often, or you want to be a billionaire with a super yacht—you still need a plan to get there. So, set yourself a little goal. Do the math. Will you be able to reach your goal through careful budgeting and raiding your piggy bank, or will it take a bit more? Do you need to take on a side hustle for a few months to fund it, or maybe the plan needs to be a bit more hard core than that. Whatever the plan needs to be:

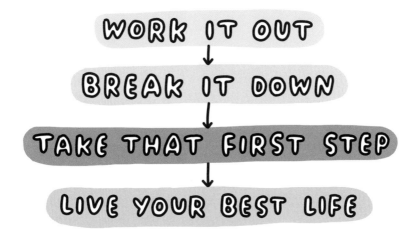

WORK IT OUT
↓
BREAK IT DOWN
↓
TAKE THAT FIRST STEP
↓
LIVE YOUR BEST LIFE

MONEY DOESN'T MAKE THE WORLD GO ROUND

UNIVERSAL FORCES DO,
AND THEY DON'T HAVE
ANY MONEY WHATSOEVER.

COLD HARD FACTS ABOUT COLD HARD CASH

Here's a few things I want you to remember about money:

Money is not the root of all evil. Money can be involved with evil things, but it is rarely the cause. For example, evil is Alan Rickman cheating on Emma Thompson in *Love Actually*. The money he spent buying his secretary a necklace isn't what was really to blame. So don't feel like a bad person for needing and/or wanting it.

Saving money isn't inherently good and grown-up, and spending money on takeaways isn't inherently bad. As with most things, balance is best.

There is just so much money in the world, there's plenty to go around. Obviously, it doesn't really work out fairly and go around evenly, but that's a much bigger topic for a whole other book. Point is, there's some out there for you somewhere. Go and get it.

It's privileged and simplistic to say "it's only money," but also, it's definitely not the most important thing in the world. There is a lot more to life than just earning money. I won't pretend that money doesn't make life a lot easier though. It opens doors. It gives you a break. If nothing else, having more money means you are in the best possible position to help make the world better for other people.

Which is why I say this with absolute certainty—it might not be easy to sort out your money shit, but it is 100% worth it.

CHAPTER 11

HOME

HOME IS WHERE

THE ~~HEART IS~~

PILE OF CLOTHES THAT YOU
HAVE WASHED YET CAN'T
QUITE SUMMON UP THE
ENERGY TO PUT AWAY AND IS
JUST WAITING FOR YOU ON YOUR
BED WHEN YOU WANT TO
GO TO SLEEP IS

HOME SWEET HOME

The idea of home is a comfortable and soothing place where you can return to and feel safe. A sanctuary. But for some people, home might not actually be a place, rather a... state of mind. Okay that sounds a bit pretentious, but hopefully you kind of get what I mean.

Working out what home means for you just makes it easier for you to find more ways to feel at home. At peace. Safe from the demands of the horrible outside world, and free from the requirement to wear makeup or any sort of remotely restricting clothing.

So dig a bit deeper into your idea of what makes you feel at home...

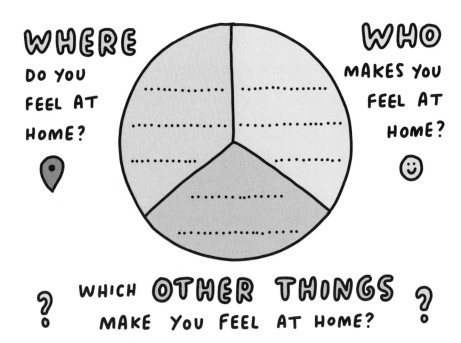

WHERE DO YOU FEEL AT HOME?

WHO MAKES YOU FEEL AT HOME?

WHICH **OTHER THINGS** MAKE YOU FEEL AT HOME?

HOME IS
WHEREVER
YOU ~~LAY~~
~~YOUR HAT~~
FEEL A BIT NICE

A HOME FIT FOR A... YOU

I'm not going to deny that I would like to live in a magical, gigantic ice palace or something similar so that all my visitors would be like "Wow, this place is so cool." But actually, the person who really needs to be happy with my home is me. (And my dog. I don't think he'd like an ice palace.) The same goes for you.

Whether you're in your forever home (lucky thing) or you're always on the move, it's always worth making your surroundings feel a bit more homely—whatever that means to you.

Do the annoying little jobs that need doing, not in case you have unexpected company (stressful), but for **your** benefit. You do **not** have to go wild and spend a fortune to make your space feel a little bit more you. Whether it's some pattern or color in the soft furnishings or just a whole bunch of cat ornaments that make your soul feel nourished, get it done.

Whatever it is that will make you feel good—do that. Don't build it all up to be some huge job that isn't worth spending any time on because you might not be there for long or because you're busy and tired. You might not be able to live in your dream home, but you deserve some dream home vibes, in whatever way is achievable right now.

DREAM HOME VISION BOARD

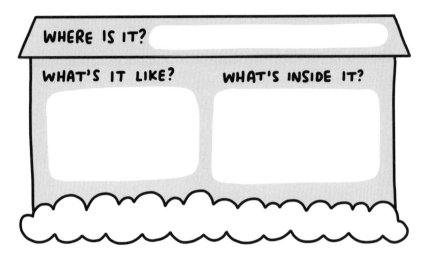

WHERE IS IT?

WHAT'S IT LIKE?

WHAT'S INSIDE IT?

♥ Remember, you can never have too many cute cushions.

☺ If home is a person and you can't be with them, then put up pictures.

♥ If home is a song, make a playlist.

☺ If home smells like pine trees and tea bags, you're going to have to spend a long time experimenting with candles. But I have every faith in you that you can do it.

♥ If home needs the sea but you find yourself landlocked, then I'm pretty sure there's a million cute driftwood signs waiting for you on the internet.

NOT QUITE LIVING THE DREAM YET? MAYBE JUST TRY TO BRING A LITTLE BIT OF IT TO LIFE AT A TIME...

IT ALWAYS
SEEMS
IMPOSSIBLE
UNTIL ~~IT'S~~
~~DONE~~

YOU HAVE ORGANIZED
A FAIR SYSTEM FOR
DETERMINING WHO
TAKES THE BINS OUT.

COHABITING IN HARMONY

In this world where your rent or mortgage is more likely to be paid in bars of solid gold than in paper money, living together is often the result of a logical decision of what makes the most financial sense rather than a romantic decision to solidify your relationship or a true, deep-down desire to experience commune living.

Successful (i.e., happy) cohabiting is going to take compromise, patience, and clearly defined responsibilities. However, I think on a human level, it kind of works. As with everything, a lot of it is finding the right other human/humans, and then the rest is about learning what each other's whole vibe is.

TIPS ON LIVING IN HARMONY

♡ We all have different preferences when it comes to daily routine, levels of mess, interior decoration, and the ideal number of cushions per square foot of sofa. All of these things impact how we want to live in our space, but they might not always line up with the preferences of the people we live with. You're gonna need to put all your ideals in a cauldron and pull out something that is the exact average of all of them. Some things you'll get to have your way, others you will have to compromise on. That's life.

☺ There's no shame in having some kind of rota or agreement to make sure everything is getting done, from buying milk to cleaning the toilet. It prevents your household from nurturing a Petri dish of bacteria and resentment.

PETRI DISH OF RESENTMENT →

♥ Agree on a little bit of give and take. Some days you might be up for cooking a fancy three-course meal for the household that uses every pan in the kitchen and four different fresh herbs. Other days you might need to walk in the door, order a pizza, and go straight to bed and eat under the duvet. We're all only human. Unless you live with some sort of robot butler, in which case just let them do everything.

WELCOME HOME HUMAN COMPANION

😊 It takes a bit of practice. You'll probably have a honeymoon period where nothing can shake your conviction that this was a good idea, and then maybe a little rocky patch where you can't think of any reasons why it is a good idea. Then hopefully you'll settle into a bit of a routine.

♥ Part of that routine is that you need some time and space just for you. If the only place you can get that is in the bath, then make sure you stake a claim on 7pm bathtime (ideally, just after someone else has cleaned the bathroom...). And make sure you give the person or people you live with their own time/full control of the TV remote control every now and again, too.

RESERVED

PHEW. TIME TO RELAX.

JUST KIDDING, YOU'VE STILL GOT TONNES OF STUFF TO DO AROUND THE HOUSE.

HOUSEWORK. IT'S ALWAYS THERE FOR YOU

JUST WAITING FOR YOU TO LOOK AWAY SO IT CAN ALL NEED DOING AGAIN IN LIKE 10 MINUTES

I can't really talk about "home" without facing up to the fact that, for most of us, home will represent at least some form of obligation to keep your space in a reasonable condition. Because that seems to be what being a grown-up is mostly about. It gives, and it takes away.

I hope for your sake that you are the sort of person who enjoys cleaning and tidying, because that will make this part of your life a lot more joyful than it is for me, a person who is not really a fan.

If you aren't a fan either, I find **little and often** is a good technique. Try and set aside a good time for yourself to do a bit every day. Whether you're an early bird who likes to push the vacuum cleaner around before you leave the house in the morning, or you're a housework demon who gets possessed just before bedtime, have that little window in mind and just go to town for twenty minutes.

Another thing that works for me is this: Just before I'm about to sit down and watch an episode of my favorite TV series, I do one extra little chore that I wasn't going to do. It's like a little bonus for my future self, and I enjoy my time in front of the TV that little bit more.

BUILDING A HAPPY HOME

Although maybe not building a house from scratch.
That always looks incredibly stressful on TV.

If you're unhappy at home, then first of all, I'm so sorry.
One of the hardest things in the world is if we don't feel happy at
home, whether that is because of the people we're living with, the
fact that we're living alone, the condition of our home, or the
amount of admin it adds to our lives. This is because it is very hard
to get away from. It can also feel like work is never done or we
want more and that stops us enjoying what we have.

DO THOSE QUICK FIXES

Spending three years saving up for a new kitchen will be much more
bearable if you spend a weekend and the cost of a tin of paint to
freshen it up a bit. Obviously you can't just paint over annoying
housemates, but you can hang fairy lights in your bedroom and make
it a nice space to hang out and plot your eventual escape.

MAKE A LONG-TERM PLAN + GET THAT GOING

Open a savings account, make a vision board for your dream
bathroom, or at least start looking at the options that will bring
you long-term happiness.

DON'T COMPARE YOUR SITUATION TO OTHERS

That's where you'll find even more misery and rage.

GIVE YOURSELF A BREAK

Okay, fine, I know that won't work. But sometimes the only thing
that helps is extremely annoying—focus on the roof over your head
for a minute, instead of the fact that it leaks a bit. (But also, once
that minute is over, I'd probably look at getting the roof fixed,
because that could be a problem.)

CHAPTER 12

FUN

YOU WEREN'T PUT ON THIS EARTH JUST TO PAY BILLS AND DIE.

I'M NOT 100% SURE OF THE ACTUAL REASON WHY, BUT IT'S DEFINITELY NOT THAT.

A COMPREHENSIVE GUIDE ON HOW TO HAVE FUN

Here's my forty-step guide to having fun, with multiple case studies, tasks, and a test at the end.

Just kidding. That's fun, right? See, it's already working.

Basically, having fun shouldn't really be a hard thing for you to do in itself. So why have a chapter on it in a book titled *How to Do Hard Things*? Well, having allowed so much of my life to get sucked up by other responsibilities and obligations to the point where taking twenty minutes to myself for a bubble bath feels like an indulgence I should feel guilty about, I understand that making time for yourself to do something that is purely for your enjoyment can sometimes feel impossible.

So I suppose, instead of dedicating this chapter to the top ten ways to have fun—which I think there is probably some disagreement on—I think I'm just going to try and convince you that you are worthy and deserving of some pleasure in your life.

If that's okay with you, of course.

GIRLS (+ EVERYONE ELSE) JUST WANT TO HAVE FUN.

AND IF THEY DON'T WANT TO, THEY SHOULD EXAMINE THE REASON FOR THIS VERY CLOSELY, TO MAKE SURE THEY HAVEN'T INTERNALIZED THE IDEOLOGIES OF CAPITALISM AND/OR THE PATRIARCHY AND TIED THEIR SELF-WORTH IN WITH PRODUCTIVITY.

SOMETIMES YOU
NEED TO
REMEMBER YOU
ARE JUST ONE
HUMAN PERSON,
NOT A SUPER
ROBOT WIZARD

(AND THAT'S OKAY.)

LEARNING TO REST

There is a whole world out there full of wild and wonderful things you can do to pass the time. But if you feel compelled to fill all your time with jobs and tasks, then you're probably exhausted and have very little enthusiasm to even think about fitting in something fun. So let's start with learning to rest.

First of all, in complete contradiction to me telling you you don't need to be productive at work—**rest actually is productive**. But the good kind, not the capitalist mandated kind. Fuck the system and all that. Resting helps you take a step back from whatever you're dealing with and return with some fresh perspective.

Physically resting and mentally resting can be quite different things. Notice when you're missing out on one. You might be getting plenty of sleep, but if your brain is racing for your every waking moment, you might need to increase your mental, not physical, rest time.

Rest should be something you look forward to. If the idea of laying on the sofa for the day fills you with dread or makes you feel all fidgety, your best form of rest might be playing rollercoaster simulator video games or going for a walk. Find what works for you.

A day of rest is a nice concept, but it isn't the only way to structure your time out. Sure, if you run yourself ragged all week, then you probably will need a whole day at the weekend doing nothing. But it is probably healthier to rest little and often.

Finally, if there is something that is going to play on your mind the whole time you're trying to rest, either try and deal with it before you settle down, or make an official plan of how you're going to deal with it after your rest.

Phew, that was a lot to read. You deserve a rest.

A COLORING/DESIGN YOUR OWN PAJAMA PAGE...
(CLEVER SUBLIMINAL MESSAGE ABOUT REST RIGHT?)

PAJAMAS

NOT DRAMAS

WHAT IF I
TOLD YOU YOU
CAN HAVE FUN
DOING SOMETHING
WITHOUT EVER
TURNING IT INTO
A BUSINESS AT
ANY POINT...

HOBBIES DON'T HAVE TO BE SIDE HUSTLES

It seems to be a thing now that if you start a hobby, inevitably, it turns into a small business at some point.

 You can't just enjoy cross-stitch. You are legally obliged to sell profane DIY embroidery hoops and get cyberbullied by incredibly furious people who have deliberately searched for your listings in order to be offended.

You can't just do yoga. You need to run a suite of wellness-themed social media accounts and subsequently make money through affiliate links to laxative teas and (hopefully stain-resistant) yoga pants.

You can't even glue crystals onto a wine glass for your own enjoyment anymore. At least, not without setting up an online marketplace and getting excessive amounts of orders and complaints from people who say your product is a rip-off and they could do it much cheaper, no problem.

I almost started a baking business once before realizing that actually, while I quite like baking, I can barely handle the pressure I put on myself for a cake to be perfect when it's just for me, let alone the added stress I would have got from selling them to paying customers.

I'm not saying that you shouldn't ever start a business based on something that started as a hobby. I'm sure that's where a lot of the most wonderful, creative, and successful businesses come from. I'm just saying, be careful you don't turn a fun escape into a hugely stressful obligation.

Being good at stuff is fun, sure, but have you ever tried being really bad at something and still enjoying it and not giving a single fuck?

BEING A BIT RUBBISH CAN BE LIBERATING

I know, it's often much easier to enjoy things once you get good at them. The first bit of learning the guitar—where your fingers are bleeding and you don't understand any of the music and even when you play something right it still sounds terrible—can be a bit of an ordeal. But if you are getting satisfaction out of your progress and feel compelled enough by the potential end result to keep going—good for you. **That's what it's all about.**

Of course, obviously, there are some hobbies where the bit where you're rubbish kind of prevents you from really doing the hobby at all. I do often wonder how you go from not being able to pole vault to being able to pole vault... The first one that goes right must feel quite spectacular.

I know it can be tempting to get competitive. One minute you're dipping your toe into running, even though you aren't much of an athlete, working your way up to running 5k with no regard for speed or aesthetic. But then you notice your colleagues posting little diagrams of how far they ran in their lunch break and a little part of you starts to feel like maybe you should be trying harder. So now, instead of bumbling along quite happily (or as happily as anyone is while running), you've got that extra little bit of pressure in your head to be better.

Sometimes, a little healthy competition is good. But if the pressure to be good at something you were previously finding fun is taking the fun out of it then, well, that kind of sucks. So in those situations, maybe instead of measuring progress, you measure your enjoyment.

STOP TRACKING YOUR RUNS

Just run for however long you want to run for. Judge a successful run by how you felt when you were doing it or how many dogs you saw on your route, instead of how far or how fast you went.

PLAY YOUR GUITAR FOR LONGER ON THE DAYS YOU GET LOST IN MUSIC

. . . and stop on the days where you just want to smash it up.

MEASURE YOUR POLE VAULTING BY...

actually, I really have no business talking about pole vaulting. Just pole vault your little heart out.

In conclusion: We miss 100% of the shots we don't take, we fail to learn every complicated instrument we give up on, and we suck the joy out of even our most favorite "escape" by turning it into a business. That's why having fun can seem hard sometimes.

So don't overcomplicate it. Think of something you find fun. Now, go and do it.

SOME DAYS YOU FEEL GOOD

BECAUSE YOU'VE *absolutely* SMASHED EVERYTHING ON YOUR TO DO LIST.

OTHER DAYS YOU FEEL GOOD

BECAUSE YOU MANAGED TO HAVE A SHOWER.

WHICHEVER IT IS, I HOPE YOU FIND SOMETHING THAT MAKES YOU *feel good* TODAY!

AFTERWORD

Wow, what a rollercoaster that was. Ironically, writing this book has been an incredibly hard thing for me to do.

Life—it's such a bloody complicated arrangement, isn't it? Sometimes, the simplest thing punches you right in the face and leaves you dazed. Other times, you solve a complex problem that leaves you feeling like you could take on the world.

While I'm incredibly proud to say I've done a lot of hard things—things I never imagined I would be able to do—there have also been things I just couldn't get the hang of. Usually, it's not because I'm incapable, but because there are a bunch of other things I need to focus on more.

There's no shame in finding something difficult, or asking for help, or even giving up. You can do hard things, but you don't have to do them for the sake of it, and you don't have to do them alone.

Whatever it is you're doing your best to do, I'm here cheering you on. And hopefully everyone else that's read this book is also cheering. The world needs a little bit more cheer.

YOU CAN DO ANYTHING, BUT YOU CAN'T DO EVERYTHING.

SO JUST ASK FOR SOME HELP OR PAY AN ACCOUNTANT OR SOMETHING.

INDEX

DEDICATION

THIS BOOK IS DEDICATED TO MY LOVELY GRANNY, EILEEN.

She made the world a brighter place,
and made the hard things seem a little bit easier.

ABOUT THE AUTHOR

Veronica Dearly is a British illustrator inspired by the many ups and downs of actual real life. Classically trained in the art of that bubble writing you learn from the person sat next to you in middle school, and self-taught in most other respects, her work is simple but recognizable. There're usually lots of clouds, too.

Born in London and raised in Slough, Veronica now lives in Devon with her husband, Craig; two rapidly growing children, Oli and Tabby; Olivia, the corn snake; and Fang, the very small fluffy dog.

FACTS ABOUT ME...

I'm left handed
I don't like cheese
I leave everything until the last minute
I love Jamiroquai, and also frogs
I always have the TV on in the background when I'm working
I love camping

Project Editor Beth Davies
Editor Vicky Armstrong
Project Art Editor Jenny Edwards
Production Editor Siu Yin Chan
Senior Production Controller Louise Minihane
Managing Editor Pete Jorgensen
Managing Art Editor Jo Connor
Publishing Director Mark Searle

Additional design work Elena Jarmoskaite

DK would like to thank Jennette ElNaggar for proofreading.

First American Edition, 2022
Published in the United States by DK Publishing
1450 Broadway, Suite 801, New York, NY 10018

A catalog record for this book
is available from the Library of Congress.
ISBN 978-0-7440-5702-7

DK books are available at special discounts when purchased in bulk for sales
promotions, premiums, fund-raising, or educational use.
For details, contact:
DK Publishing Special Markets, 1450 Broadway, Suite 801, New York NY 10018
SpecialSales@dk.com

Printed and bound in China

For the curious

www.dk.com

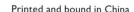